Being a Muslim in the World

Other Palgrave Pivot titles

G. Douglas Atkins: T.S. Eliot Materialized: Literal Meaning and
Embodied Truth

Martin Barker: Live To Your Local Cinema: The Remarkable Rise of
Livecasting

Michael Bennett: Narrating the Past through Theatre: Four Crucial Texts

Arthur Asa Berger: Media, Myth, and Society

David Elliott: Fukushima: Impacts and Implications

Milton J. Esman: The Emerging American Garrison State

Kelly Forrest: Moments, Attachment and Formations of Selfhood:
Dancing with Now

Steve Fuller: Preparing for Life in Humanity 2.0

Ioannis N. Grigoriadis: Instilling Religion in Greek and Turkish
Nationalism: A "Sacred Synthesis"

Jonathan Hart: Textual Imitation: Making and Seeing in Literature

Akira Iriye: Global and Transnational History: The Past, Present, and
Future

Mikael Klintman: Citizen-Consumers and Evolutionary Theory:
Reducing Environmental Harm through Our Social Motivation

Helen Jefferson Lenskyj: Gender Politics and the Olympic Industry

Christos Lynteris: The Spirit of Selflessness in Maoist China: Socialist
Medicine and the New Man

Ekpen James Omonbude: Cross-border Oil and Gas Pipelines and the
Role of the Transit Country: Economics, Challenges, and Solutions

William F. Pinar: Curriculum Studies in the United States: Present
Circumstances, Intellectual Histories

Henry Rosemont, Jr.: A Reader's Companion to the Confucian *Analects*

Kazuhiko Togo (*editor*): Japan and Reconciliation in Post-war Asia: The
Murayama Statement and Its Implications

Joel Wainwright: Geopiracy: Oaxaca, Militant Empiricism, and
Geographical Thought

Kath Woodward: Sporting Times

DOI: 10.1057/9781137301291

palgrave▸pivot

▶

Being a Muslim in the World

Hamid Dabashi

palgrave
macmillan

DOI: 10.1057/9781137301291

BEING A MUSLIM IN THE WORLD
Copyright © Hamid Dabashi, 2013.

First published in 2013 by
PALGRAVE MACMILLAN®
in the United States—a division of St. Martin's Press LLC,
175 Fifth Avenue, New York, NY 10010.

Where this book is distributed in the UK, Europe and the rest of the world,
this is by Palgrave Macmillan, a division of Macmillan Publishers Limited,
registered in England, company number 785998, of Houndmills,
Basingstoke, Hampshire RG21 6XS.

Palgrave Macmillan is the global academic imprint of the above companies
and has companies and representatives throughout the world.

Palgrave® and Macmillan® are registered trademarks in the United States,
the United Kingdom, Europe and other countries.

ISBN: 978-1-137-30130-7 EPUB
ISBN: 978-1-137-30129-1 PDF
ISBN: 978-1-137-30128-4 Hardback

Library of Congress Cataloging-in-Publication Data is available from the
Library of Congress.

A catalogue record of the book is available from the British Library.

First edition: 2013

www.palgrave.com/pivot

DOI: 10.1057/9781137301291

For the memories

of my mother's silent prayers

and my father's loud protests

DOI: 10.1057/9781137301291

In the name of God, the Beneficent, the Merciful

Hast thou observed him who belieth religion?

That is he who repelleth the orphan

And urgeth not the feeding of the needy.

Ah, woe unto worshippers

Who are heedless of their prayer;

▶ *Who would be seen (at worship)*

Yet refuse small kindnesses!

The Holy Quran, chapter 107, Al-Ma'un/Acts of Kindness

DOI: 10.1057/9781137301291

Contents

palgrave▸pivot

DOI: 10.1057/9781137301291

Introduction: Muslims in the World

Civilization: The West and the Rest—who would write a book with a title like that today, and what could it possibly mean? The British historian Niall Ferguson has made a reputation for himself for theorizing "the West" as the defining disposition of humanity at large. But like many other latter-day ideologues of the beleaguered empire, Niall Ferguson is more a panegyrist of "the West" than its prognosticator.

If the idea that "science, medicine, or work ethic" were the virtues and achievements that civilizations around the globe lacked before "the West" appeared on the horizon was offered in a sophomoric essay in any half decent college, the idiocy would earn a much-deserved F for the student. But why is it that when offered by an historian it receives a bravura publication? The answer has to be in the realm of the mass hysteria that these sorts of ideas generate at the world-historic moment when this very "West," as an idea, is witnessing its own demise. That we are living through "the end of Western ascendancy," so far as Ferguson thinks he is the harbinger of that good tiding, is a splendid thing—for that "ascendency" was predicated on mass murder and mayhem from one end of the earth to the other (including the European Holocaust), and on the global plundering of planetary resources. The word "civilization" in Ferguson's title is the giveaway—the unabashedly racialized self-congratulation that before this "West" there was no civility, and that after the "West's" demise it will die. As a categorical imperative, "the West" is dying, and that is a good thing—for that means the world is delivered from one of the ghastliest imperial projects ever historically coined and experienced. As for science, medicine, literature, philosophy, and such—what "the West" picked up from previous empires and expanded upon will survive its demise and be carried over into the new global formations of the world. Upon that world, people—including Muslims—will now have to imagine themselves in a post-Western history that is finally delivered from one particularly troublesome delusion.

To be in the world

"The West" is no more—and nor are, a fortiori, all the binaries it has coined and crafted over the last two hundred years plus—chief among them the notion of "Islam" that Orientalism invented for the West. "The West and the Rest" was the language of the European and American imperialism at the height of the normative hegemony that crafted "the West" and subjugated "the Rest." Niall Ferguson and his ilk come at the tail end of that narrative fiction. Financially bankrupt (look at Greece, the fictive birthplace of "the West"); politically corrupt (look at presidential elections in the US); economically stagnant (look at the US debt to China); and diplomatically inept (look at the Iranian nuclear issue), all signs indicate that this thing Niall Ferguson still calls "the West" has long since imploded—with post-modernism and post-structuralism as its paramount philosophical eulogies.

What does it mean to be a Muslim in this post-Western world? What world will Muslims inhabit in post-Western societies, in or out of the Muslim world as we have hitherto understood, defined, and located it? In what way can even we talk about a Muslim world, and how is that world different, integral, or embedded in other worlds? Doesn't the end of "the West" as a self-asserted criterion also mean the end of Muslim world as it was manufactured in liaison with that divisive category?

To have a world means to have an attitude toward it, as Gadamer noted in *Truth and Method* (1960), and that attitude is linguistically mitigated. As a historian of endangered species, Niall Fergusson is a museum piece, a dying specimen of what he desperately celebrates, the chronicler of a world that no longer commands our attention. I write this book in the exact opposition of his direction. He writes to extol the centrality of that

DOI: 10.1057/9781137301291

"Western" figment of his imagination—I write in the aftermath of the calamity that this term and, what it stood for, visited upon the world. He mourns the decline of that West—I celebrate it. He mourns the decline of an imperial adventure that made his race feel triumphant; I sing the praise of the people I call my own—from Asia to Africa to Latin America—who survived its terror with tenacity, creativity, and courage. The imperial conquest of the world that kept calling itself the "West," not dissimilarly to other globalized empires—from the Achamanids to the Abbasids to the Mongols—has fortunately come to an end, and the globalized condition of the capital that has befallen the planet no longer has any one particular empire in control. The Americans, Europeans, Russians, or the Chinese may think they are in control—but they neutralize each other, and a mass democratic uprising, open-ended precisely because its outcome is uncertain, has forced history into a new point of origin. "The West" no longer has either a military, moral, or normative command over anyone's credulity. Nostalgia for a defeated world must perforce yield to embracing and celebrating the one that is surfacing. Being a Muslim in the world means to come to terms with the emerging post-Western world that is rising beyond the power and hegemony of the last empire.

The "Islam" that "the West" needed and gave birth to a set of twins that match each other perfectly: we must decouple those twins as we recognize the coupling of Osama bin Laden and Ayaan Hirsi Ali as the binary opposites of militant Islamism and rabid Islamophobia that both require each other and cancel each other out. As we leave this couple in the company of Niall Fergusson, and bid them all well to sort out their differences, a vast and more widely open world is open to us in which to wonder and figure out how is it possible to be a Muslim in the world.

The outline of an argument

The first task Muslims face is actively to imagine ourselves in a world liberated from the "the West" and all the false binaries it has generated and sustained. In chapter 1, "But There Is Neither East nor West," I posit the question of what it means to be a Muslim in the world in the context of the collapsing of "the Islam and the West" binary. The transition requires the crafting of a new language for coming to terms with Islam, and it no longer matters if it is in Arabic, Persian, German, or English, as long as that language is in conversation with the emerging, not the disappearing,

DOI: 10.1057/9781137301291

world. What matters is the paramount hermeneutic necessity that the *particularity* of that language is stipulated within its presumed or intended *universality*. That universality is changing, and the sooner we begin to reconfigure the language that Muslims speak in relation to that emerging universality, the better. The time is in fact urgent and fast upon us. The language of "Islam and the West," as the language of "religion versus secularism" has exhausted itself, slammed into a cul de sac, and with the decline and implosion of "the West," the emerging diction of Muslims must flower into its own universality, a universality embedded in the global context of our worldliness.

Imagining ourselves in a post-Western world requires the dismantling of the *regimes of knowledge,* the fiction "the West" has historically generated. In chapter 2, "Breaking the Binary," I explore why a post-Western regime of knowledge is necessary and how in fact its elements are already evident. The habitual binaries between "Islam and the West," between "religion and secularism," need to be discarded. These binaries have concealed more about Muslim worlds than they have revealed about them. They have been imposed by the power of regimes of knowledge production that take "the West" as an *ontological a priori* and narrate the rest of humanity in terms conducive to that primacy ("The West and the Rest"). The language of "Islam and the West" secured, from its very inception and in its very grammatology, a condition of superiority for one and an epistemic vicariousness for the other side of the imbalance. Breaking that binary is a critical task we must undertake by way of retrieving the worlds that preceded it.

There is no better way to dismantle the dominant regimes of knowledge than by retrieving the pre-colonial condition of cosmopolitan worldliness Muslims historically experienced. In chapter 3, "The Muslim Cosmopoles," I argue that being a Muslim in a post-Western world requires a critical rethinking of Islamic cosmopolitanism as Muslims lived it over many centuries. An active recollection of what that cosmopolitanism entailed—one in which "secularism" means nothing—enables possibility of inhabiting the renewed worldliness of Muslims' lived experiences. Europe's "Enlightenment modernity" became a falsely universalized concept under colonial duress. Its otherwise parochial provincialism as a domestic European event reached a cul de sac of its own in the aftermath of the European Holocaust and the onslaught of post-colonial struggles that followed, and thus scarcely has anything to say about, or to, humanity at large. The form of the thinking about Islam

DOI: 10.1057/9781137301291

and of being a Muslim in the world will not be abstracted from this condition unless Muslims are located in the particularity of the end of that condition of post-coloniality.

A key factor in retrieving pre-colonial Muslim worldliness is the historical agency of the Muslim who does this retrieving. In chapter 4, "Being a Muslim," I argue that being a Muslim in the emerging world is both an ontological question and a proposition predicated on a radical rethinking of the epistemic terms with which new regimes of knowledge might take shape. The formalism of the critical and creative faculties necessary to cultivate a language of existential self-awareness is contingent on the formal disposition of the language we will have to cultivate in conversation with the vital parameters of our renewed pact with post-Western history. That formality will have to be deeply rooted in our lived experiences today—particularly critical given that we need to silence the noise of the daily news to experience the timbre of our time. "If every language represents a view of the world," Gadamer suggests in *Truth and Method*, it is "because of what is said or handed down in this language."[1] What is said and handed down in the language of "Islam and the West" is what we need to overcome. The chief obstacle to that overcoming is the rampant Islamophobia of our time that determines the terms of engagement with the world—a task that I propose in this chapter must be overcome before we are free to decide the terms of our own interiority, exteriority, worldliness, and above all to be able to retrieve our intuition of transcendence.

To come to terms with the world in which Muslims live requires a radical reconsideration of the relation between this and the other world—the sacred sanctity that governs Muslims' worldliness. In chapter 5, "*Din, Dowlat, and Donya*: Rethinking Worldliness," I ask how the terms *din* and *dowlat* can be separated. What does it mean to ask for a secular politics, divorced from people's sacred certitudes? By going back to the Arabic/Persian words *din* (religion), *dowlat* (state), and *donya* (world), I raise the linguistic horizon we need to revisit as we come ashore to a new globality of our consciousness. We need to rethink these concepts for, as Gadamer noted, "a view of the language is a view of the world...Language is not just one of man's possessions in the world, but on it depends the fact that man has a world at all."[2] In that language, the forced binary between a tyrannical theocracy and a militant secularism is a false choice.

We cannot escape asking the critical question of "religion" and what it means in the context of this renewed engagement with the world.

DOI: 10.1057/9781137301291

In chapter 6, "Religion—Quote Unquote," I turn to the word "religion," and ask how we may come to terms with what that concept entails and the alterities implicate. The world exists as a world because of the worldly disposition of the language that facilitates the reading of that world as a lived experience. "Not only is the world 'world' only in so fast as it comes into language, but language, too, has its real being only in the fact that the world is re-presented within it." That Gadamerian insight will have to guide us to a renewed conception of "religion." "The fundamental linguisticality of man's being-in-the-world," as Gadamer puts it, demands the necessity of that hermeneutic encounter. The linguisticality of the "Western world" was predicated on a relation of power between the West and the Rest—and thus the necessity of the emergence of a language that is at once conscious of itself and corresponds to the post-Western world.

Finally, in my conclusion I bring all these strands together to argue that being a Muslim in the world requires asking an existential question in the bosom of a worldly religion that has all its otherworldly aspirations deeply rooted in the one we fearfully embrace and must wholeheartedly trust to hand it over to our children. This world and its fragility require a renewed pact, a planetary self-reflection, a manner and mood of entrusting itself to itself. Thinking through this possibility requires a new agency I wish to identify with the category *a Muslim intellectual*, rooted in a renewed organicity that must be conscious of its worldliness.

Notes

1   Hans George Gadamer, *Truth and Method* (New York: Continuum, 1975): 399–400.
2   Ibid: 401.

DOI: 10.1057/9781137301291

1

But There Is Neither East nor West

Abstract: *In Chapter 1, I posit the question of what it means to be a Muslim in the world, in the context of the collapsing "Islam and the West" binary. This transition requires the crafting of a new language for coming to terms with Islam, and it no longer matters whether it is in Arabic, Persian, German, or English, as long as that language is in conversation with the emerging, not the disappearing, world. The language of "Islam and the West," as indeed the language of "religion versus secularism," have exhausted themselves, slammed into a cul de sac; and with the decline and implosion of "the West," the emerging diction of Muslims must flower into its own universality, a universality embedded in the global context of our worldliness.*

Dabashi, Hamid. *Being a Muslim in the World.*
New York: Palgrave Macmillan, 2013. DOI:
10.1057/9781137301291.

Estimates are that some 1.6 billion human beings living on this earth identify themselves as Muslims. But beyond their ritual prayers and other obligations of faith, beyond their common belief in a set of doctrinal principles (chief among them the Unity of God, the sanctity of the Holy Qur'an, the nobility of Prophet Muhammad, and the certainty of a Final Resurrection and Divine Judgment), what else does it mean for them to be Muslims? They are told they have a proud and noble heritage, and yet they face, and in fact are integral to, a rapidly disintegrating human habitat. Beyond any degree of piety that they might hope and anticipate for their posterity, what sort of Muslims would they dream their children to be in this world, and framed in this very history they live?

Indeed, how is it possible for a Muslim child—whether Afghan, Iranian, Arab, Turk, Pakistani, Indonesian, American, European, Latin American, or African—to grow up with a sense of rootedness, belonging, moral and intellectual responsibility to, in, and for this world? It no longer matters if you live in Cairo, New York, Damascus, London, Tehran, Tokyo, or Dakar: being a Muslim in the world requires rethinking the world Muslims inhabit—around 60% of them in the Asia-Pacific, 35% in the Middle East and Africa, around 3% in Europe, and just about 0.3% in the Americas. Muslims are everywhere—but where in the world are they?

"Islam and the West"

The casting of Islam against the West—both essentialized and forced to the polar ends of an immaterial binary—has, ever since the European colonial encounter with Muslims, posited a proverbial "Islam" against a falsifying category code-named "modernity," camouflaging the inner logic and rhetoric of a worldly religion that is yet to rediscover its own tropes of multiple and varied historic encounters with its alterities.

Today, in their new worldly globality, Muslims must decouple their communal faith from the delusional apparition of "the West," and at the same time stop indulging in the fake and futile binary between their "tradition" and a "modernity" that for them was a colonial construct. After a two-hundred-year-plus encounter with colonial modernity, the inner logic of that European project has imploded, and Muslims are finally free to re-imagine themselves anew in the world.

With the rise of European and then American imperial adventures, Muslims have been at the receiving end of other worldly empires

DOI: 10.1057/9781137301291

(collectively code-named "the West") that have forced them into a self-alienating dialogue. Under the spell of non-Islamic imperial settings, Muslims have continued to be conscious of themselves, to be sure, of what and who they are, but it is a false, defeated consciousness, formed under duress, resulting in Muslims being unable to recognize themselves in the mirror of those other empires. There is a cognitive dissonance in the historical memory of Muslims to be the subject of successive imperial settings not their own. From the Umayyads and the Abbasids early in Islamic history to the Ottomans, the Safavids, and the Mughals at the dawn of European colonial modernity, Muslims have been the defining moments of world historic empires. The task today is not the delusional fantasy of retrieving those empires but to recollect the cosmopolitan worldliness that thrived under those empires, now necessary to be recast into a new globality—a task not to reinvent another Muslim empire, but to resist any and all empires. In that resistance dwells the new worldliness of being a Muslim the world.

The Eurocentric project of modernity against which Muslims have had to recognize themselves was from its very inception a *colonial modernity*, with no universal validity or force to it beyond its battleships and fighter jets, violent means of domination that have in fact exposed its bellicosity and revealed its belligerent nativism that insists on universality—wiping out the moral maps that faced and challenged its claims to global validity. The task facing a world in which the underbelly of the false universalizing urge of the thing that calls itself "the West" is to actively retrieve worlds that have been concealed and falsified under the distorting questions that European *modernity* or *secularity* keeps asking from those worlds—with and through concepts and categories entirely alien to peoples and cultures from Asia to Africa to Latin America, except when they have faced the gun barrel of European (and then American) colonialism and imperialism, in other words, modernity and secularity under duress.

The urgent task facing contemporary Muslims is to bring their worlds to self-consciousness beyond the self-alienating encounter with European colonial modernity and in the context of the new worldliness that Muslims (like all other people) face. During their encounter with colonial modernity, Muslim intellectuals themselves—from Muhammad Abduh (1849–1905) to Ali Shari'ati (1933–1977)—systematically and consistently reducing their own multifaceted cosmopolitanism into a solitary site of ideological resistance to colonialism. This was not the Orientalists' task. But now, in the wake of a global uprising—from the Green Movement

DOI: 10.1057/9781137301291

in Iran to the Arab Spring, the Eurozone crisis unrest from Greece to Spain, and the widely globalized Occupy Wall Street movement—the world is on the verge of a renewed awareness of itself. In this context, Muslims need to be equally instrumental in retrieving a past that will cast them as agents in their future beyond that falsifying binary of "Islam and the West."

To be a Muslim in the world today does not require an Islamic *reformation*, as some have suggested. Quite the contrary: it requires the *restoration* of Islam back into its worldly disposition, remembering its conditions of pre-coloniality to deliver itself from the conditions of post-coloniality. If Osama bin Laden and Ayaan Hirsi Ali represent the two extremes of militant Islamism and virulent Islamophobia, respectively reading Islam back and forth into a fictive past and a pathological present—the restoration of Islam into its worldly disposition means entrusting Muslims with the emerging and pressing task of being-in-the-world. Islam has always been the dialogical outcome of Muslim collective consciousness engaging in conversation with the dominant moral and intellectual forces in the world—from a position of power. Having been for over two centuries at the receiving end of European and American imperialism, and having turned their faith into a singular site of ideological resistance to those empires, Muslims will now have to retrieve that habitual dialogue, though not from a position of power but from a position of *care*—care of the other, of the world, that will in turn redefine who and what they are.

"Islam" as a sign

In this new world, as Islam as a signifier is categorically released from its "Islam and the West" binary, Islam has lost its chief nemesis and interlocutor of the last two hundred years, and when "Islamism" as a political ideology has been effectively exhausted, and the new globality of Islamic presence requires a different mode of multiple and parallel dialogues, when the face and the fact of *the other* of being a Muslim-in-the-world will have to be the site and citation of Muslims' emerging worldliness. If the traumatic events of 9/11 were the end of Islamism as a militant ideology, the Arab Spring is the commencement of this new dispensation. The assassination of Osama bin Laden and the Islamophobia evident in the Western European and North American celebration of Ayaan Hirsi Ali

DOI: 10.1057/9781137301291

are the mutually destructive sites of the emerging dialogue of Muslims with their posterity—spoken in the language of the hope they have invested in their children in the ideologically liberated global context. It is not enough to say that Osama bin Laden did not represent Muslims; nor is it sufficient to say that Ayaan Hirsi Ali is an Islamophobe. Muslims need to live a life in defiance of both those pathologies—by inhabiting the world that is much in need of their *care*.

Today Muslims around the globe look at their children and can only imagine, and must dare to dream, the language of liberation their offspring have already started speaking.

To come to terms with the specifics of that global context we must locate the sign of "Islam" where it has been most maligned. From the public pronouncements of such prominent and powerful figures as the former US President George W. Bush, former UK prime minister Tony Blair, and Pope Benedict XVI to the erudite musings of some of the most distinguished European philosophers, such as Jürgen Habermas, Slavoj Zizek, and Umberto Eco, a binary opposition between an ahistorical "Islam" and an equally essentialized "West" has disproportionately determined the language and disposition of almost everything that is politically consequential for encounters between two major components of humanity at large—two components that have already dissolved into the making of a globalized fragility far beyond their fictive boundary.

To alter the terms of public conversation about Islam in both its immediate regional and global contexts, I put forward the proposition of *Islam in the world* via the active agency of *Muslims-being-in-the-world* by highlighting two interrelated but pervasively neglected intellectual domains. At the heart of this idea rests the simple proposition that throughout its long and multifaceted history, Islam has always been in creative, critical, or even combatant conversation with one or another major and effectively "global" interlocutor. This historical fact has given Islam a quintessentially *cosmopolitan* and *dialogical* disposition.

In the forced binary manufactured between "Islam and the West" under colonial duress Muslims as Muslims are deprived of agential autonomy to worldliness—the world in which they find themselves is already determined. In this essentialist distinction, maintained not just in the public domain but also even in much contemporary "critical" thinking, "Islam" is often posited as a monolithic and entirely ahistorical proposition, while "the West" is presupposed in equally categorical and definitive terms—having attained in fact an ontological disposition.

DOI: 10.1057/9781137301291

Thus, "Islam" and "the West" alike become catatonic fixtures of moral authenticity and normative measure beyond cultures and conditions, civilizational premises outside the fold of world history, as readily cherished and celebrated by some as demonized and denounced by others. My emphasis here on the intellectual diversity, cosmopolitan organicity, and organic *historicity* of Islam directly repudiates the fallacious and dangerous fabrication and propagation of these dominant and exceedingly dangerous binaries—the last, lingering, vestiges of a colonial and colonized imagination.

Once posited in such binary and oppositional terms—and against a massive body of scholarship on both "Islam" and "the West," respectively, that underline the historically specific nuances of such categories and thus effectively undermine their generic essentialization—Muslims lose all their internal dynamism, geographical expansiveness, heterogeneous cultural dispositions, doctrinal variations, sectarian tendencies, and above all, their prolonged historical developments and trajectories. The very first Islamic dynasties, the Umayyads (651–750) and then the Abbasids (750–1258), were formed in combatant battles with the Sassanid and Byzantine imperial institutions, imaginations, kingship theories, moral and intellectual underpinnings, and political practices. In the domain of enduring ideas and intellectual institutions, a similar dialectic has been at work. In gradual conversation with classical Greek thought, the vast and multifaceted aspects of Islamic philosophy took shape. In both subtle and overt exchanges with Jewish theology, various schools of Islamic theology were elaborated. In similar exchanges with Christian asceticism, Hindu and Buddhist Gnosticism, and Neoplatonic philosophy, Islamic mysticism (Sufism or Irfan) emerged. In eventual conversation with Pahlavi and Sanskrit literatures, Arabic as well as Persian, Turkish, and Urdu canons of literary humanism (*Adab*) developed. Following exposure to Greek, Indian, and Chinese philosophies, various disciplines in Islamic sciences developed. Finally, and most immediately evident for contemporary purposes, following the various Muslim encounters with European colonialism and Enlightenment modernity, a diverse range of ideological movements and political perspectives (politcial Islamism, Third World Socialism, and anti-colonial nationalism) came to preoccupy Muslim thinkers and define the modern Islamic world—always in dialogical and progressively unfolding terms.

To rethink Muslims in the world, we need to remember the creative cultures of medieval Islam and how their dialogical dispositions were

DOI: 10.1057/9781137301291

conducive to the eventual creation of a multifaceted, syncretic, and poly-focal civilization. We need to recall a broadly historical perspective that demonstrates the cosmopolitan character of the Islamic civilization in its varied forms and manifestations. We must pay particular attention to the rise of literary humanism (*Adab*) in its Arabic, Persian, Turkish and Urdu contexts. We need to re-imagine the rise of major multicultural urbanism in Muslim lands—in Damascus, Baghdad, Cairo, Istanbul, Cordoba, Isfahan, and Delhi, in particular—as the principal sites of these cosmopolitan cultures. In making the case for the prevalence of this cosmopolitanism we must mark the territorial and material basis of Islamic civilization

The goal is to retrieve the internal dynamics of Islam itself, breaking it down to its discursive, institutional, and symbolic forms—all competing with one other, each remembering Islam anew as the constitutionally cosmopolitan culture that it has always been, and thus dialectically deny-ing any one component of this multifaceted religion the presumption to assume a dominant, exclusionary, or defining moment. *Polyfocal* has always been the discursive disposition of Islam, just as the languages and cultures through which it has spoken are *polyvocal*, and the geographical domains and domesticities of its historical manifestations are *polylocal*. The polyfocality of Islamic epistemic cultures has spoken and written itself in conflicting *nomocentric* (the law-centered Shari'ah), *logocentric* (the reason-centered Falsafah), and *homocentric* (the human-centered *Tasawwuf* or *Irfan*) languages and lexicons. The centrality of Arabic lan-guage in varied expressions of Islamic thought has had to contend with equally powerful traditions of the same in Persian, Turkish, and Urdu (and now, one might add English, French, German), or any of the other languages spoken by Muslims around the globe—thus giving a distinctly polyvocal disposition to Islamic discourses, all mapped out in a geo-graphical polylocality that has profoundly impacted where and when a Muslim speaks one or another particularly powerful scholastic diction.

My principal argument here is that only under dire political circum-stances does one of these discourses (the nomocentricity of the Islamic law in particular) assume an overriding claim over the entirety of Islam, and always at the heavy expense of repressing, denying, and thus dis-torting the factual cosmopolitanism of Islamic historical experiences. In arguing and unfolding this lived experience of Islamic moral and imaginative history, we will retrieve the idea and practice of an Islamic cosmopolitanism that weds its characteristically multifaceted orientation

DOI: 10.1057/9781137301291

to an increasingly globalized world which has hitherto assigned to Islam either a retrograde or even an intrinsically fanatical disposition, either a "moderate" or a "radical" nature. Given the rapid globalization of a notion of Islam negotiated between two modes of extremism—one systematically demonizing it, the other categorically reducing it to a militant juridicalism, the articulation of Islam in its historically anchored cosmopolitanism is an urgent concern for a large global audience.

The defining disposition of Islam in its encounter with European colonial modernity has been the generation of a succession of cosmopolitan cultures that embraces and includes Islam in its varied forms and doctrinal expressions, but that is not reducible to Islamic doctrinal principles in general or to juridical mandates in particular. Here we need to make a distinction between "Islam" in its doctrinal foundations in the Qur'an and the Hadith literature and its juridical character in Islamic law (Shari'ah), on one hand, and "Islam" as a lived experience that covers a vast range of symbolic, discursive, and institutional domains, on the other. The characterization of a society, thus, as "Islamic" certainly includes the fundamental beliefs and practices of its inhabitants as Muslims but is by no means limited—and might in fact be contrary—to such *doctrinal* principles and practices. Muslim worldly experiences thus reemerge as the locus classicus of a vast and diversified body of cosmopolitan mores and practices, ranging from the sacred to the mundane, and as such, remain irreducible either to narrowly Islamic or anti-Islamic, religious or anti-religious, sacred or secular, "Western" or anti-Western. Both demographically and culturally, the existence of Jewish, Christian, Hindu, and Buddhist communities alongside Muslim ones has not been incidental to what we categorically call "the Muslim world," but in fact definitive of it.

Remembering the time past

We need to retrieve a view of the vast and diversified Islamic heritage that is irreducible to Islamic doctrinal beliefs—placed within successive worldly empires, until it reached the European imperial context, and has now, in the age of a globalized condition of the Empire, emerged from that context too. Positing Islam as a cosmopolitan worldliness, and doing so in a way that will have a conclusively transformative impact on the way we ordinarily think of the terms "Islam" or "Islamic" are

DOI: 10.1057/9781137301291

the contours of the task facing us in the age when post-coloniality as a condition of knowledge production has come to an end, a proposition I developed in detail in my *Arab Spring: The End of Postcoloniality* (2012).

The diversified Islamic heritage I propose here is predicated on *a hermeneutics of alterity* rather than *a politics of identity*. That hermeneutics of alterity, which I propose has always been definitive of Islamic intellectual history and worldly experiences, has been categorically eclipsed and compromised by the politics of identity imposed on Muslims under colonial duress, and in that state of colonial duress, Muslims themselves have been instrumental in that fateful transmutation of their own collective integrity. "Islam" has never been a reduction of Muslims to what the Sunnis and the Shi'is have thought of each other, or what mystics and philosophers have said about each other. Islam has been the metamorphic sublimation of the constellation of those dialectics, and never the tribal reductionism of that constellation to one sect or another. Islam has been a hermeneutics of alterity sublated to a *gestalt view* of Muslims of themselves. It is precisely that gestalt view, predicated on a hermeneutics of alterity, that needs to be retrieved today.

I propose this view of Islamic societies as a fundamental challenge to the very categorical division of the world into an East-West axis—an axis that has historically distorted our free and democratic understanding of world history far more than it has facilitated such an aspiration. We do not need a "dialogue of civilization"—we need the dissolution of civilizational thinking along the inherited East-West binaries altogether—and to do so we need to retrieve that sense of worldliness in which Islamic or any other civilization was narrated in order to transcend themselves. Both "the clash" and "the dialogue" among civilizations exacerbate what in fact needs to be dissolved and overcome—the divisions of a fragile humanity along tribal fault lines. I also target this principal argument of my work against newly emerging calls for an "Islamic reformation"— based on entirely unexamined assumptions that disregard the integral history of Islam itself. What Muslims need for the full realization of their global citizenship, against both political demonization from outside and fanatical reductionism from within is not a belated "reformation" but a vibrant *restoration* of their own enduring historical cosmopolitanism— recast within the current worldly parameters.

In specifically ideological terms, the almost simultaneous formation of *anti-colonial nationalism, transnational socialism,* and *political Islamism* in combative encounter with European colonialism is the clear

DOI: 10.1057/9781137301291

manifestation of a multifaceted political culture that is at once domestic to Muslim political experiences and yet deeply influenced by global factors and forces. I propose the formation of these discrepant and profoundly powerful ideological forces over the last two centuries and throughout the Muslim world as the clear indication that the cosmopolitan disposition of Islamic societies is ipso facto irreducible either to "Western" or "anti-Western" influences and forces. What is lost, what is hidden, under these false binaries is precisely the cosmopolitan worldliness we need to retrieve.

My primary purpose here is to posit a reading of Islam as a cosmopolitan world culture, which in both its lived experiences and normative dispositions is integral to a liberating humanism. That humanism is inimical to any mode of tendentious tribalism, "Islamic" tribalism in particular. I will thus read (Islamic) "tradition" in this context to be the most potent invention of (European) "modernity," completing the decisive binary opposition by which the "universal" claims of European Enlightenment are shown to be far more metaphysically posited than inherently warranted. European Enlightenment modernity will whither and waste on the jagged edges of its colonial legacies, while it may yet regain potency and momentum from a creative conversation with Islamic cosmopolitanism.

The natural habitat of Islam—as evident in its long and pervasive history, in both its medieval and modern phases—is a worldly setting. Thus, of necessity, any exclusionary, monolithic, and politically dominant "Islam" is in fact a historical and epistemic aberration that becomes ideologically contentious only under severe political circumstances, particularly when it is positioned in a politically combatant mode against an imperial adversary. We must therefore trace the mutation of the cosmopolitan Islam into militant Islamism back to its historical encounter with European colonial modernity, when Islam was systematically reduced—above all by its own leading ideologues and public intellectuals (from Jamal al-Din al-Afghani and Muhammad Abduh, through Sir Seyyed Ahmad Khan and Rashid Rida, down to Mawlana Mawdudi and Ali Shari'ati)—to a monolithic site of ideological resistance to foreign domination.

By disengaging "Islam" and "the West," we need to restore to *both* Islamic and Western European/ North American cultural dispositions their respective and inherently historical dispositions, irreducible to one faith or another, without disregarding the enduring significance of these faiths in the polyfocal pluralism of these cultures. The intention

DOI: 10.1057/9781137301291

in this reading of Islam is to resituate world history on a leveled field of fair and open remembrance and conversation, but not between two fictive apparitions ("Islam and the West"), but in terms domestic to the lived experiences of people, in the material and lived domain of their collective experiences—all categorically removed from the entrenched ideological and overtly political tribalism of one sort ("Islam") or another ("the West").

The idea I propose here is deeply destructive of our received and deeply internalized discursive formations. The very narrative juxtaposition of "tradition" versus "modernity," or "Islam" and "the West," or "secular" versus "religious" has in fact cross-essentialized and deeply antagonized two powerful figments of imagination that in their political renditions have wreaked havoc on our world by depriving historically syncretic, pluralistic, and cosmopolitan cultures of their defining moments and historical character. The generation of an enabling civic discourse in the public domain, I contend, is impossible to imagine without this disengagement.

The significance and urgency of this reorientation in thinking for informed public debate about some of the most vital contemporary issues of our time can hardly be over-emphasized or exaggerated. As a worldly religion, Islam has now been turned and mutated into a sign and sig-nifier of unbridled and vicious violence. Millennial bodies of original sources in science and philosophy, literary humanism and scholastic learning, along with generations of scholarship and sustained com-mentary in multiple languages, have now all lost the public domain to a politically manufactured notion of Islam as entirely synonymous with the most wanton disregard for the abiding norms of civility, nobility, or even decency. There is no one in particular to blame in this state of affairs, and yet no one in particular can be exempted from responsibility to restore historical depth and moral imagination to the term "Islam." We have reached a stage at which it is now exceedingly difficult even to imagine, let alone to convince an ordinary citizen in North America or Western Europe, that Islam was once the designation of a worldly civility and continues to be the defining measure of decency and self-respect for more than a billion human beings around the globe. Restoring the historic cosmopolitanism of Islam as a worldly religion to its contempo-rary configuration and thus thinking through its inherent pluralism and hybridity is not merely a matter of intellectual duty but also of immedi-ate civic responsibility.

DOI: 10.1057/9781137301291

A world liberated from the "the West" and all the false binaries it has generated raises anew the question of what it means to being a Muslim in a vastly altered context. The paramount hermeneutic necessity of raising that question is rooted in uplifting its *particularity* towards a self-conscious *universality* that will have to reconfigure the manner in which Muslims speak, and for which manner of speech they need neither permission from any colonial officer, nor authorization by any post-colonial theorist.

DOI: 10.1057/9781137301291

2
Breaking the Binary

Abstract: *In Chapter 2, I explore why a post-Western regime of knowledge is necessary and how in fact its elements are already evident. The habitual binaries between "Islam and the West," between "religion and secularism," need to be conceptually discarded. The language of "Islam and the West" has secured, from its very inception and in its very grammatology, a condition of superiority for one and an epistemic vicariousness for the other side of the imbalance. Breaking that binary is a critical task we must undertake by way of retrieving the worlds that preceded it, and anticipating what is coming next.*

Dabashi, Hamid. *Being a Muslim in the World.*
New York: Palgrave Macmillan, 2013. DOI:
10.1057/9781137301291.

On Friday morning, March 23, 2012, I met with a delegation of Egyptian revolutionaries visiting Columbia University for a conference organized by a number of law students at our university. The success of the Egyptian January 25, 2011, revolution was on everyone's mind, though the paramount concern of our guests that day was the political ascendency of the Muslim Brotherhood in the newly elected parliament. The new parliament was about to draft a constitution that would be heavily influenced by what was termed "their Islamist agenda," and our Egyptian friends feared their civil liberties would be very much limited within the confinements of the Islamic Shari'ah. When they realized I was not as concerned as they were and solicited my opinion, I responded that the active formation of voluntary associations—such as labor unions and women's rights organizations—was the key revolutionary agenda at hand, and that this would be the way for them to resist any potential tyranny, rather than simply wishing that the Islamists, or any other emerging political bloc, would guarantee their civil liberties. In a not-so-hyperbolic moment, I turned to a member of the delegation, a young woman much respected among her peers as a key figure at the Tahrir Square, and I asked, are you not a Muslim? She said, sure, she was. I said, why don't you go to your local mosque and organize your community around a common concern? The mosque belongs as much to you as to the local Muslim Brotherhood. The key factor here, I suggested, is to overcome the false and falsifying binary between *the religious* and *the secular* and to reclaim Egyptian society with a renewed civic definition of itself.

Searching for God in all the right places

I am not sure how much sense I made to our Egyptian guests at Columbia. But I remain convinced that the binary opposition between the secular and the religious is one of the most effective forces pre-empting the possibility of overcoming our colonial and post-colonial mindsets.

But how are we to overcome that mindset?

What we need is not a political argument, but a hermeneutic imagination in excavating some key concepts in our moral and intellectual heritage. Consider the Persian word *kharabat,* which has quite a convoluted origin. Persian literary historians have concurred that the word originally meant a "house or tavern of ill repute" but was eventually appropriated by the mystics to mean a place that they frequent by way of suspending all

DOI: 10.1057/9781137301291

hypocritical pretense to piety.[1] Among its possible etymological roots, we may consider the word *kharabat* to be a combination of two exactly opposite words: *kharab* and *abad*, or "ruinous" and "prosperous," respectively. The idea is that there are places that you can frequent that will dismantle your beliefs, and yet, in doing so, will also restore your faith. The proverbial tavern in Persian poetry is that kharabat.

Dar kharabat-e Moghan nur-e Khoda mibinam (In the Magi's ruinous tavern I see the light of God).[2] Hafez is in a house of ill repute, a tavern where gamblers and drunkards gather, and even more scandalous, he identifies this place with the infidel Zoroastrians. He relishes the evident shock of seemingly irreconcilable paradoxes. He sees God where debauchery thrives. The poetic persona who narrates Hafez's lyrics is incorrigible, worldly, wise, and wondrous—lives to drink wine and be merry—and in the midst of that, not despite it, he sees God. He loves music, and is not much fond of scholastic disputations. Much more can be added to the list of his mischievous behaviors, but—and here is the rub—he is a Muslim. His nom de plume means "he who knows the Qur'an by heart," and in his poetry he boasts that he can recite it with fourteen different interpretations. "Would I ever stop drinking in the season when flowers bloom / How could that ever is, when I boast of a superior intellect?" That is Hafez—or the persona who sings and dances in his lyrics. He sins, thrives in sinning, and yet does so not despite being a Muslim but *as* a Muslim.

There is a worldly disposition to and about Hafez (1326–1390), a material matter-of-factness, within which he dwells and from which he derives his faith. He loves beauty, drinks wine, boasts of a superior intelligence for doing so; he loves to listen to music; willingly spends his fame for asceticism and knowledge to be joyously in the company of singers and musicians; he is not much fond of scholastic learning, yearns to be with the persons he loves, and is not sure how long he will be in this world—yet he is not afraid of the long list of sins that he will have accumulated by the time he meets his creator, for he is convinced of the divine grace that will forgive a much longer list of sins than he could ever gather in a lifetime. He is on this earth by virtue if that divine grace, and he will return to it—of that he is sure.

So: was Hafez not a Muslim?

One can randomly pick any poet, prose stylist, historian, philosopher, mystic, or scientist from any point in Muslim history and ask the same question. There is a disconnect between the cosmopolitan universe

DOI: 10.1057/9781137301291

of Muslims, from South Asia to North Africa into Muslim Spain, that existed before their encounter with European colonial modernity and its aftermath. Whence this disconnect?

I offer the word *kharabat* as the simulacrum of the world I have in mind when I suggest worldliness as the locus classicus of the emerging Muslim whereabouts—a paradoxical location, impure and yet precisely in its impurity the place of salvation, where God can be located. The world is a *kharabat*, and yet upon it shines the light of God—so says Hafez, and so must we come to terms with that superior wisdom.

Overcoming the secular

In the proverbial aftermath of 9/11, the world seemed fixated on how to resolve "the problem of Islam." From a world religion, Islam had now mutated into a global problem. Atrocious acts of violence randomly perpetrated by a handful of Muslims were categorically severed from the even more violent context of United States/Israeli warmongering, and instead of a close reading of the historical circumstances that occasioned those acts of violence, Islam as a religion, in the entirety of its multifaceted, multicultural, and polyfocal reality, was put on an essentialist pedestal and examined in public (usually by people least qualified to do so) for the peculiarity of its proclivities to violence. The panacea that usually under these circumstances was offered is the process known as *secularization, modernization,* or even *Westernization.* Muslims, it seems, have to become other than what they are to be considered civilized and non-violent. The question then becomes, to what degree are Islam and, by extension, Muslims receptive to change, to these generous acts of secularization, modernization, or Westernization, offered them by the proverbial (Rudyard Kipling's) White Man.

Now that, after two successive US-led wars in Afghanistan (since 2001) and Iraq (since 2003), for every innocent American murdered on 9/11, thousands of equally innocent Muslims have also been murdered, we may revisit the question of secularization anew.

The problem of secularization (or modernization, or Westernization—the White Man's burden of civilizing the world)—is predicated on the assumption and designation of the unexamined term "Islamic societies"—on first calling certain societies "Islamic" and then awaiting or designing a process of delivering them from that predicament through "secularization." The

DOI: 10.1057/9781137301291

term "Islamic societies" is an entirely Orientalist designation— aided and abetted by nativist Muslim intellectuals facing up to the reality of European colonialism, or else wishing "to secularize" their societies in tandem with it—posited not against Christian (or Jewish, Hindu, etc.) societies, but against a figment of imagination called "the Western societies." The Orientalist fabrication of the term "Islamic civilization," the provenance in which "Islamic societies" are placed (in conjunction with similar terms, "Indian civilization," "Chinese civilization," etc.) was meant to counter, corroborate, and dialectically upstage the presumption of "Western civilization" and perforce "Western societies," inventions of the European bourgeoisie meant to separate itself from medieval European aristocratic dynasties and ecclesiastical orders. The Orient, where "Islamic societies" were located, became the contemporary citation of a pre-modern European past—now Europeans could denounce and dismiss their own past and other people's present at the same time.

The construction of "Islamic societies" was definitive to the Orientalist project—and overcoming that designation is predicated on the historic rise of a condition of knowledge production we may call post-Orientalist.[3] Edward Said's *Orientalism* (1978), his epistemic deconstruction of Orientalism into the power relations that occasioned it, fell squarely within the already established analytical parameters of the sociology of knowledge, which, at least since Nietzsche and Marx and certainly after him Max Scheler, Karl Mannheim, George Herbert Mead, and, of course, most successfully, Michel Foucault, has addressed the problems of the social construction of "reality." Primarily because of a systematic disregard for the theoretical traditions from which Said's *Orientalism* was launched, within the Orientalist circles proper Said's text soon assumed an iconic status; there were reactions to it for or against, made regardless of the theoretical foregrounding of its principal propositions in the wider domain of the sociology of knowledge.

The globalizing agenda of imperialism (now led by the United States and hotly contested—in both political and economic terms—by China, Russia, India, Brazil, and Europe), has now surpassed its colonial and post-colonial phases, and Orientalism too has given way to a post-Orientalist mode of knowledge production. While the neo-Orientalists are busy ignoring Said's text, a closer reading of it inevitably leads to the necessary recognition that the series of issues Said raised in the colonial act of the Orientalist knowledge production falls, not only in the larger analytical context of the sociology of knowledge, but also, and more importantly, within the even

DOI: 10.1057/9781137301291

more critical context of post-metaphysical, post-epistemological, post-representational, post-structural, post-foundational, post-colonial, and ultimately, post-modern debates.

As a result, any modest and preliminary attempt toward a hermeneutics of post-Orientalism must inevitably begin by addressing the issues that Said raised, not only in the analytical context of the sociology of knowledge, but also in the more critical anti-frame of our irreversibly post-Nietzschean thinking. The unplugging of the metaphysics, the dismantling of epistemology, the anti-foundationalism of the exposure of the historical relations between knowledge and power are among the leading critical forces that today demand full attention in any hermeneutics of post-Orientalism. In short, Said's *Orientalism* successfully placed the epistemic act of reading "another culture" in its political context. The problems he diagnosed must now be reformulated and linked to the larger hermeneutic problem of reading any *other* text, any *other* culture. If we simply consider cultures as only half-materialized texts (or texts as the exegetical unfolding of cultures), then the problems of reading cultures become identical with the overriding problems of not only cultural but also textual hermeneutics.

The overriding binary between *Islam* and *secularism* does not hold; branding certain societies as *Islamic* and then narrating a troubled course of *modernization* or *secularization* for them—while they are under colonial duress—is in fact the principal conceptual source of the problem. We can go through a sustained course of discursive sites that cannot be identified as either "secular" or "Islamic," and yet they are definitive to what Orientalists have called "Islamic societies." Consider terms such as "Islamic art," "Islamic sciences," "Islamic poetry," or even "Islamic philosophy"—they are all categorically flawed, for the adjectival "Islamic" (in the strict sense of the term) does not do justice to the epistemic and aesthetic foregrounding of these disciplines and dispositions, nor indeed does "secularism." Muslims are artists, poets, scientists, and philosophers—but that fact does not make the art, poetry, science, or philosophy they do "Islamic," any more than Marxism or psychoanalysis or quantum physics are "Jewish" because Marx, Freud, and Einstein were Jews. We know Marx as a political economist, not a Jewish political economist; Freud as the founding father of psychoanalysis, not the Jewish founder of that discipline; and Einstein as an astrophysicist, not a Jewish astrophysicist. Then why should Avicenna be called a Muslim philosopher, or Hafez a Muslim poet? Neither "Islam" nor "secularism"

DOI: 10.1057/9781137301291

does justice to the philosophy or poetry Avicenna or Hafez practiced. They were Muslim, and one was a philosopher and the other a poet. That factual state of being is what needs to be configured.

Even cursory familiarity with the social and intellectual history of these "Islamic societies," from medieval to modern times, clearly demonstrates the vast and pervasive operation of a cosmopolitan imagination within them that is irreducible to anything exclusively "Islamic" in the doctrinal sense of the term; nor do they warrant the term "secular." The trouble is not with these discourses and disciplines, from philosophy to poetry, of knowledge production. The trouble is with these terms, with this false binary. The term "Islamic societies" is the product of the Orientalist imagination— branding, consuming, and alienating things from the vantage point of the Orientalists' location. Only in London or New York do people eat Chinese, Mexican, or Lebanese food. In China, Mexico, or Lebanon, people don't eat Chinese, Mexican, or Lebanese food. They just eat food. That simple fact, the universality embedded in any particular, is what is lost when we term something "Islamic" to distinguish it from "secular" or "Western."

What is a hermeneutics of alterity?

To question the validity of the terms "secularism" or "Islamic societies" is, first and foremost, to break the false binary, and then to work toward a testing ground for a theoretical proposition that in a very preliminary way one might call a *hermeneutic of alterity*. A hermeneutic of alterity is the principal theoretical concern, one of a number of "weak strategies" (as Gianni Vattimo would say) that we may explore through a subversive juxtaposition of the overriding assumption of the term "Islamic societies" against the sources of cosmopolitan imagination prevalent in these societies. When we question the supposition that "the Islamic societies" and "secularism" are a binary set of oppositions, we are in effect putting forward an argument for the pervasive and transhistorical presence of cosmopolitan imagination in the heart of Islamic consciousness in order to mobilize enough material, or, to be more exact, the historical congregation of constructed realities, when we explore the promises of a hermeneutic of alterity as a possible way out of the crisis of Orientalism, a crisis that is only an acute symptom of an even more serious problem of *foundational* and *metaphysical* thinking—you are either this or that, never the fusion or the negation of the two.

DOI: 10.1057/9781137301291

The problem with Edward Said's diagnostic reading of Orientalism arises from its very strength. By exposing the Foucauldian power relation at the basis of the Orientalist production of knowledge, Said left unattended the far more vexing hermeneutic issue of metaphysical thinking operative in Orientalism. It is certainly necessary, but by no means enough, to demonstrate the colonial premises of the production of "the Orient." The far more enduring problem, however, is how a post-metaphysical mode of knowledge could be produced while nativist movements from inside and neo-conservative strategies from outside continue to frame any liberating hermeneutic move within an East-West binary. Orientalism was not just the ideological arm of colonialism. It was equally a manifestation of a positivist streak in the European project of Enlightenment. This darker side of the Enlightenment was left completely unexamined by Said, in a considerable part because of his own humanist attachments to the project. In this respect, he is far more on the side of a Habermassian salvaging of the project of European modernity than on a Foucauldian side of a radical destruction of it. The question for us, after Said, is how to dismantle the Orientalist project beyond its political demise. There is a far deeper epistemic issue of identitarian metaphysics at work that needs overcoming.

The problem with such terms as "secularism" or "Islamic societies" is in their *ontological* supposition of a metanarrative that is to be universally applicable to a vastly fragmented world. Deeply rooted in the Hebrew Bible and the Gospels, Islam is a religion that originated in Arabia and within its first century spread quickly into Africa, Asia, and Europe. Today, Muslims live in the four corners of the world, on every continent, in numbers ranging from a rapidly growing minority in North America to the overwhelming majority of the population in Middle East and North Africa. If it ever had any claim to legitimacy, the categorical term "Islamic societies" is even less legitimate in a world fragmented along religious, ideological, ethnic, and economic lines. As a metanarrative, then, the term "Islamic societies" is a highly dubious proposition not only in its medieval application but, particularly, in its contemporary extensions as well. Overcoming fabricated binaries imposed on them, Muslims need a hermeneutic of alterity that defines who they are in *appositional*, not *oppositional*, terms organic to their worldly realities. A Muslim painter, or a Muslim Marxist, or a Muslim feminist, is an *appositional* construct, and does not implicate an *oppositional* binary. A Muslim can be a feminist, a Marxist, or a psychoanalyst, not despite

DOI: 10.1057/9781137301291

being Muslim but precisely by virtue of being Muslim. The apposition implicates both terms of the constructs and equally enables them.

As an epistemic attribution of a generic characteristic to a singular civilization, the term "Islamic societies" is an invention of the Orientalist imagination under specific historical circumstances. Egypt, Iran, or Pakistan, are not "Islamic societies." They are just societies. It is only in university departments of Oriental or area studies in Western Europe or North America that they become "Islamic societies." To understand why the term "Islamic societies" was applied to a vastly fragmented body of medieval history, we need to look at its binary opposite, the "Western societies." As a set of binary oppositions, the twin terms of "Islamic societies" and "Western societies" are coterminous, and both are the result of the European project of post-Hegelian Enlightenment. From Hegel, the European Enlightenment project learned a teleological movement of human history toward progress and emancipation. Hegel saw himself as the anticipated consequence of Plato with the same degree of fictional continuity that he saw Napoleon as the anticipated consequence of Alexander the Great. Hegel and Napoleon thus became the two epistemic and political parameters of a fictive narrative that linked the Greeks and Romans to the Enlightenment, a "European" project. The European bourgeoisie needed to link itself via the Renaissance to the ancient Greeks in order to construct an Enlightenment history for itself independent of both the fragmented aristocracies that had mapped the medieval history and the transnational Christendom that had given that history its metaphysical legitimacy. They needed the "Dark Ages" in their distanced past, as they needed "Islamic societies" (the Orient) in their immediate geography.

With the collapse of the economic foundations of European feudalism, and as Kant, Hume, Mill, Smith, and Rousseau (chief among others) began to articulate the ideological consciousness of the European bourgeoisie, medieval Christianity could no longer hold the emerging class together. Medieval Christianity had painted itself into the corner of European aristocratic feudalism. The Enlightenment project thus emerged as the revolutionary ideology of the European bourgeoisie. The generic term "the West" surfaced from the depth of the European project of Enlightenment in order to give historical and ideological validity to a bourgeois class particularly anxious to carve an identity for itself independent of both the aristocracy and the clergy. As palaces and churches increasingly turned into sites of antiquarian curiosities, music

DOI: 10.1057/9781137301291

halls, opera houses, and museums emerged as the new sites of what was now called "Western civilization."

The capitalist mode of production, in the meantime, along with the Industrial Revolution, and the increasingly powerful European bourgeoisie, soon began to extend the logic of its economy into colonialism. Inexpensive raw material, cheap labor, and the potential expansion of markets soon set the European bourgeoisie on their colonial conquests. The project of Orientalism commenced as the ideological justification of European colonialism. The figure of Napoleon, Hegel's champion, in Cairo, with an officer at one side and an "Egyptologist" on the other perfectly represents the function of Orientalism as the ideological arm of colonialism. The function of Christian missionaries in the Orientalism project should not be totally disregarded. Medieval Christianity very soon began to recast its feudal disposition and make itself useful to the emerging project of colonialism. The considerable presence of Christian missionaries among the earliest generations of Orientalists testifies to that fact.

The term "Islamic societies" was thus invented by Orientalists, and by extension by the European project of Enlightenment, precisely to designate a site of civilizational oddity at a time when the European bourgeoisie sought to distance itself from its own historical heritage by buttressing it with a severance from its geographical surroundings. While Christian missionaries saw in Islam an old medieval enemy, the Enlightenment project detected in it an alternative form of Christianity. What the Christian missionaries and the ideologues of the Enlightenment shared was an absolute that "Islam" represented an alien, civilizational Other against which "the West" was now to become self-conscious, self-assertive, and self-evident. Foucault's proposition that the formation of mental asylums was concomitant with the formation of the European idea of Reason during the Enlightenment project thus needs to be augmented in colonial terms with the simultaneous formation of the so-called Islamic societies so that Reason could find a place to deposit its counterpart idea of "un-Reason." Mad European pariahs had to be incarcerated in mental asylums just as "fanatic" Muslims had to be located in "Islamic societies" (the Orient) so that the European ideas of Reason and Progress and the Enlightenment project of capitalist modernity could be placed squarely in its fictive home on the Atlantic rim between Western Europe and North America.

To this day the term "the West" is synonymous with capitalism and its colonial claims on the world, irrespective of geographical location,

DOI: 10.1057/9781137301291

whether Japan in Asia, South Africa in Africa, and Israel in the so-called Middle East. It has been the nature of imperialism—from its pre- to its post-colonial periods—to essentialize other cultures (wipe the alternative maps of the world) to justify conquest, reversing the political rule of "divide and conquer" to "essentialize and master." As the political project of colonialism, for example, stirs the Sunni-Shi'i differences to its own advantages, Orientalism, colonialism's ideological arm, essentializes an ahistorical "Islam" to facilitate its colonial inscription. As Derrida observed about Levi-Straus's anthropological project, an "anthropological war" accompanies the colonial project; it is an observation equally applicable to the European project of Orientalism.[4] Thus Christopher Columbus can be considered the real father of anthropology because some of his descriptions of Native Americans are absolutely indistinguishable from an entire genre of anthropological studies. In the words of David Spurr in *The Rhetoric of Empire*, "the very process by which one culture subordinates another begins in the act of naming and leaving unnamed, of marking on an unknown territory the lines of division and uniformity, of boundary and continuity."[5]

To take the term "Islamic societies" to task is to retrieve these suppressed relations of power that were conducive to its historical formation and unexamined epistemic validity.

Rethinking "Islamic societies"

A critical reconsideration of the term "Islamic societies," however, must be launched toward a radical destination far beyond a mere challenge to a major Orientalist construction. We must begin to work our way toward a hermeneutics that will be different from the monolithic assumptions inherent in the matter-of-factness of that term. Let us map out that road.

Looking through that map, we may argue for the necessary theoretical and methodological substitution of an alternative mode of counter-conceptualization about communities of the sensibilities hitherto identified as "Islamic societies." By "counter-conceptualization," I do not mean to argue for the substitution of a rhetoric of "non-Islamic societies" or, worse, "secular societies." That superficial level of engagement with the problem would inevitably engage us in an equally essentialist and representationalist mode of operation that would lead us nowhere. Instead, we must reach for a careful undoing of *the metaphysics of identity* at the

DOI: 10.1057/9781137301291

root of such unexamined assumptions as "Islamic societies" and subvert it through the active agency of *a hermeneutics of alterity.*

Let me explain this distinction a little further.

We must begin by asking ourselves by what authority, that is, through the active agency of what political forces, has the master narrative of "Islamic societies" constituted itself.

I offer a counter-narrative under the rubric of "worldly imagination." A panoramic view of historical societies in which the Qur'anic memory has played a major role reveals that the holy Muslim scripture had to be staged in the context of other, equally powerful, memories. In this panoramic view, we see the acting out of diverse forces of patently anthropocentric imagination that have historically animated these societies. Privileging the sacred imagination that has been equally present in these societies, the term "Islamic societies," among a host of other, similar, megaterms of power and domination, has spread a wide and outreaching net, claiming its putative constitution and disposition, and thus successfully submerging the active agency of forces that have negated and countered it.

The retrieving of the terms of worldly imagination in the so-called Islamic societies, will have a number of immediate consequences worth noting at the outset. Should we be successful in mapping out the terms of these worldly engagements with the anxiety of being in the so-called Islamic societies, and right before we turn our attention to our ultimate destination, which is to argue, through the invocation of what Gianni Vattimo has called *il pensiero debole*, for an hermeneutics of alterity to displace the dominant metaphysics of identity, we will pause for a moment to reflect on certain moral and political issues that will have been raised by the theoretical reconstitution of the terms of worldly imagination in these societies. A successful account of the terms of worldly imagination in what we have so far received as "Islamic societies," will inevitably define and set the agenda for a number of serious reengagements with the very metaphysical assumptions of our operative historiographies on and about these societies. We will come to realize that the hegemonic appellation "Islamic societies" is a principally political proposition that privileges one side of an historical interface—between the sacred and the mundane—over the other. This political act of privileging one side of an historical debate over its contestant must be recognized for what it is, and its ideological presuppositions ought to be overthrown and dismantled. We will equally be forced to trace the roots and origins of

DOI: 10.1057/9781137301291

worldly imagination in the historical and existential experiences of these communities themselves. If indeed we are successful in demonstrating the historical presence of modes of cosmopolitan imagination in communities so far identified as "Islamic," then we can argue for the existence of a continuous, almost uninterrupted, history in the multifaceted confrontation between the worldly and the sacred imaginations in the widest and most pervasive senses of the terms.

One crucial result of this act of hermeneutic confrontation should ideally be the final suspension of the hegemonic rule of the myth of "the West" as the final arbiter of historical realities that perpetually paint "other-societies" into a "non-Western" corner, there to give troubled legitimacy to anxieties such as "The Decline of the West," "The Clash of Civilizations," "The West and the Rest," "Islam and the West," "The End of History," and other such amusing tales of which Oswald Spengler was the most successful—while Samuel Huntington, Bernard Lewis, and Francis Fukuyama have been the most recent, if not so successful—storyteller.

Significant as these crucial issues are, they fade in comparison with my ultimate contention here, which is to suggest the possibility of an alternative way of looking at these societies through a hermeneutics of alterity. Actively conscious of its hermeneuticity, that is, of its being an *il pensiero debole*, this hermeneutics is meant to substitute the self-assured, logocentric, patriarchal metaphysics of identity that, constitutional to the positivist spirit of the Orientalist project, informs and sustains the hegemonic assumptions of such conceptual categories as "Islamic societies." My insistence on the active presence of a worldly imagination in the so-called Islamic societies is thus meant, more than anything else, to act as a rhetorical device to propagate this hermeneutics of alterity.

I propose actively substituting the underlying metaphysics of identity, upon which the twin peaks of Orientalism and philology have historically rested, with a hermeneutics of alterity that makes proxy concepts, surrogate suppositions, and permanently provisional propositions a counter-constitutional habit. Permanently substitutional, all propositions made in a hermeneutics of alterity are always on a standby status, acting as their own surrogates, their own potential understudies, with replacementarity being their chief counter-virtues. Oscillating between the two replacementarity of the sacred and the mundane imaginations, which is at once both and neither, is the ironic mode in which this counter-narrative operates. Read in this way, individuals operate not in two exclusionary spaces of the sacred or the worldly, but on the

DOI: 10.1057/9781137301291

active continuum of fictive/rhetorical bipolarities that unite and negate both. The supposition of any ontological access to the historical making of these, as any other, societies must commence with a simultaneous abandonment of all illusions of metaphysical certainties operative in such conceptual categories as "Islamic societies" by actively cultivating the post-metaphysical, anti-representational groundlessness, Vattimo's *il pensiero debole*, of multiple claims on historical allegiances of individuals, always politically anchored, never practically irrelevant.

As a methodological proposition, the crucial significance of this act of deconstruction must be clearly understood. The critical undoing of "Islamic societies" as a monolithic master term, leading to the archeological excavation of its Orientalist roots, is an imperative act of de-essentialization from which no hermeneutics of post-Orientalism has any escape. The so-called "strategic use of a positivist essentialism in a scrupulously visible political interest," as Gayatri Spivak has put it, may indeed function well for that particular political end. But as Spivak herself in fact repeatedly points out "[a] strategy suits a situation; a strategy is not a theory," [6] and as a result any—even, or perhaps particularly, strategic—act of cross-essentialization has doubly dangerous implications for the sort of work we need to do in our post-Orientalist crisis.

All our (substantive and strategic) critical work must be entirely targeted against both the epistemological and the political assumptions of essentialism—"Islam" and "The West" chief among them. The construction of "Islamic societies," as indeed the very capital construction of "Islam" itself as a masterwork of cross-historical validity (without any regard for the historical forces operative in the relentless acts of existential re-constructions of innumerable number of Islams) was the handiwork of a great essentializing act in the Orientalist project both in its epistemological (philological) and political (colonial) underpinnings. As a major political mistake, any cross-essentialization of "Islam" and/or "The West" will continue to produce the catastrophic consequences of nothing beyond name-calling, without any hope of escaping from the paralyzing implications of the effective end of Orientalism as a colonial project. This task, first and foremost, must be carried forward by Muslims themselves, for it was Muslims themselves who effectively transferred the legacy of their historical thinking into a discursive disposition against European colonialism.

With this colonial background in full view, the deconstructive strategy against the Orientalist project and its essentialist construction

DOI: 10.1057/9781137301291

of archetypical "Islamic societies" should ultimately be informed by a recognition of the metaphysical underpinnings of such constructs and, in Gianni Vattimo's terms, their "violent" categories. Substituting these "violent" categories, following Vattimo's reading of Nietzsche and Heidegger, with "weak" ones, or what he calls *il pensiero debole* (or postfoundationalist thought), is a critical step out of the post-Orientalist crisis, as we must work our way toward a hermeneutics of post-Orientalism. Let me quote Vattimo here so that the relevance of the strategy of *il pensiero debole* in an anti-Orientalist act constitutional to the construction of a hermeneutics of alterity becomes more evident:

> As Nietzsche had seen very clearly, and as Heidegger shows in ontological terms, the metaphysical tradition is the tradition of "violent thinking." With its predilection for unifying, sovereign and generalizing categories, and with its cult of the arché, it manifests a fundamental insecurity and exaggerated self-importance from which it then reacts into over-defensiveness. All the categories of metaphysics are violent categories: Being and its attributes, the first cause, man as "responsible," and even the will to power, if that is read metaphysically as affirmation or as the assumption of power over the world. They must be "weakened" or relieved of their excess power.[7]

There are no better terms than "excess power" or "violent thinking" to convey the epistemological and political tyranny with which terms such as "Islamic societies" have imposed their hegemonic acts of conditioning over a vast spectrum of social-existential experiences. The post-metaphysical act of undoing "Islamic societies" as a categorical assumption of universal significance thus seeks to retrieve, via a strategy of *il pensiero debole*, the contradictory/animating forces of those communities of sensibilities in which varieties of Qur'anic memories, among the festive and ferocious congregation of other, non-Qur'anic, memories, have had a role to play. It is not at all clear why the strong humanist traditions in Arabic, Persian, Turkish, or Urdu literary legacies should be any less privileged in having a defining status for those communities of institutionalized and creative sensibilities in which they have had a major role to play.

The strategic adaptation of Vattimo's conception of *il pensiero debole* must become operative in the pragmatist context of anti-representationalism (best stated by Richard Rorty), which is particularly helpful in any act of thinking seriously engaged in rhetorical deconstruction of the Orientalist project, by far the greatest gesture of hegemonic representation in modern history. The monolithic supposition of "Islamic societies" has postulated a truth-claim by virtue of which the metanarrative

DOI: 10.1057/9781137301291

of "Islam" is believed to have had an overriding role in the history of a major universal civilization. The term "Islamic civilization" has thus come to occupy the necessary opposite pole of the other great fiction of modernity, "Western civilization."

To oppose the enduring reign of that metanarrative one must begin with a radical reconsideration of any mode of knowledge "not … as a matter of getting reality right," to quote Rorty, "but rather as a matter of acquiring habits of action for coping with reality."[8] There is this absolutist positivism about the Orientalist project, deeply rooted in its colonial roots, which considers an ahistorical conception of "Islam," remarkably akin to that of the most committed clericals who have an historical class interest in assuming so, as the sole and defining arch category of any society—from Morocco to Indonesia—in which some version of the Qur'anic memory has found a place. The vast spectrum of cultural coming-to-terms with reality—which obviously includes that Qur'anic memory but is not reducible to it, is thus reduced to an archetypal assumption about "Islam" and its absolutist and universal claims to what Vattimo would rightly consider "violent" (categorical) moral and political authority.

Following Vattimo's lead in *il pensiero debole*, a hermeneutic of alterity must be able to unlearn all the serious epistemics operative on the basis of the metaphysics of identity and begin to relearn a Bakhtinian kind of carnivalesque and work its subversive forces into its operation. Something of the free and festive celebration of the Bakhtinian subversive notion of the carnivalesque must become operative at the very heart of a hermeneutic of alterity as it works its way out toward an effective dismantling of the reigning metaphysics of identity at the roots of the Orientalist project. Identity in the sense that there is serious belief in a notion of "the West"— which is monolithic, ahistorically valid, and as if always present—and a simultaneous belief in a sister notion that there is "the East"—which is equally, however conversely, so—must be dismantled via an alterity that recognizes centrifugal forces historically in operation, thus ipso facto undoing the illusion of centralizing (totalitarian) identity. Substituting the Bakhtinian carnivalesque for a Hegelian Geist, we must keep Nietzsche's only half-joking quip in mind: "Supposing truth is a woman. What then? Are there not grounds for the suspicion that all philosophers, insofar as they were dogmatists, have been very inexpert about women? That the gruesome seriousness, the clumsy obtrusiveness with which they have usually approached truth so far have been awkward and very improper methods for winning a woman's heart."[9]

DOI: 10.1057/9781137301291

In all *un*seriousness, in a hermeneutic of alterity, a built-in Ibsenian supposition of "on the other hand" is always there to subvert the slightest suggestion of inadvertent dogmatism that it itself might tend to harbor. Parsing ways between self-mockery and self-celebration, and thus able to laugh at itself freely, oscillating between the opposing ends—two or many—of all manners and metaphors, of all histories and stories, and on the wide and transgressive margins of those enabling doubts that love and hate their certainties with equal passion is where a hermeneutic of alterity rests its case, hangs its cause, places its bets, and feels most at home.

A hermeneutic of alterity subverts its own traces of crypto-metaphysics evident in its apparent claims to hermeneuticity by the compromising forces of "a hermeneutic" (i.e., one among many historically conditioned acts of readings), of a lower-cased "hermeneutic" (having no claim to totalizing acts of power-based readings: an act of reading as a simultaneous invitation to others), of "hermeneutic" in the singular (thus denouncing all pretensions of systematicity), and ultimately, by the rhetorical privileging of "alterity," that is, the anti-metaphysical, anti-epistemological celebration of ironically institutionalizing anti-institutionality. Constantly operating on both ends of any metaphor, a hermeneutic of alterity works its way to reading/making reality through the self-mocking, ironic mode visible in its own trademark, wherein the pseudo-metaphysics of hermeneuticity sits next to the self-subversive force of alterity. The result is launched toward a counter-methodology that detects and celebrates cultural heteroglossia in all its acts of reading cultures as carnivals.

A hermeneutic of alterity is thus an always already tentative attempt not to abandon the project of reading and knowing (whether texts or cultures, or more accurately, culture/texts) altogether, but stay the course against all odds. It is one among many possible experiments with a potential reading of cultures in a post-metaphysical, and in our case, post-Orientalist, mode. The base of pressure and emphasis is much more on "alterity" here and now than on "hermeneuticity" as a modality of knowing. The built-in, self-mocking, ironic form of *alterity* present in a *hermeneutic of alterity*, in conspiracy with the disclaiming strategy of "a hermeneutic" with no claim to totalizing systematicity, forces any hefty supposition in "hermeneutic" out of its crypto-metaphysical tendencies. The counter-metaphysics of alterity prevents all acts and suppositions of objectivism and seriousness, and the weak proposition of "a hermeneutic" guards against self-defeating relativism and frivolity (as Richard

DOI: 10.1057/9781137301291

Bernstein and Garry Madison have done with Rorty and Derrida). If my "weak" and weakening proposition of "a hermeneutic" is charged and informed by Gadamer's Hermeneutics, then my insistence on "alterity" is deeply committed to the Derridian deconstruction, with the Bakhtinian carnivalesque as the meeting ground between these two opposing claims.

De-totalizing the world

The construction of "Islamic societies" as a hegemonic category claiming to explain just about everything about societies in which the varieties of Qur'anic memory, among a constellation of other non-Qur'anic memories, have had a role to play, owes its totalizing origin and legitimacy more than anything else to the over-Islamicizing tendencies in the Orientalist project. The particular reasons, causes, and consequences of this totalizing enterprise are yet to be examined in the historical foregrounding of the Orientalist project itself. Whatever its causes and circumstances, the Orientalist project gave metahistorical authority to the adjectival "Islamic" to sit in front of practically all cultural, social, and political dimensions of these societies.

As a totalizing claim, however, the epistemic category "Islamic" conceals much more than it reveals about the effective histories of these societies. The point of contention here is not to dispute the fact that what is habitually referred to as "Islamic civilization" is principally, but by no means totally, the work of people who self-consciously recognized themselves as Muslims. Nor is it to deny the equally compelling fact that in many significant respects the cultural, social, and political dimensions of this civilization are traceable to the enduring and unfolding significance of the Muhammadan charismatic event and his Qur'anic revelations. Nor, indeed, is it to point to the significant presence of non-Islamic—principally pre-Islamic Arab, Greek, Hebrew, Syriac, Iranian, Indian, and even Chinese—forces in "Islamic civilization." To the degree this civilization was "Islamic" it borrowed and assimilated quite a number of significant cultural traits into the bosom of the hermeneutic unfolding of its Qur'anic memories. The point of contention is, instead, to question that degree or even nature of *Islamicity* and ask whether the *totalizing* categorization of "Islamic" does justice to the internal and syncretic dynamics, forces of self-contradictions. and dialectical disposition that constitute these so-called Islamic societies.

DOI: 10.1057/9781137301291

What the term "Islamic societies" conceals more than anything else is the unresolved, if indeed it can ever be resolved, bipolarity of the sacred and the mundane imaginations as they center their respective narratives around the defining moments of theocentricity and anthropocentricity, respectively. The crucial tension between theocentricity and anthropocentricity in the sacred and secular imagination is the chief unresolved problematic of these, and indeed many other, societies. By privileging the sacred imagination over the mundane and the worldly (both integral to each other), the Orientalist project in effect sided with the clerical institutions, subsumed the worldly humanism constitutional to these societies, and represented a monolithically "religious" society in its construction of "Islamic history"—without ever allowing the term "religious" to disconfigure itself. Among many factors that may explain this Orientalist proclivity toward the clerical, as opposed to patently non-clerical, institutions is the deep roots of the project in Christian missionary zeal and the fact that quite a number of leading Orientalists were devout Christians. But equally responsible for the Orientalist privileging of the religious over the worldly is the fact that as a colonial project Orientalism was deeply rooted in the Enlightenment project and its celebration of Reason and Progress. "Islamic societies" had to be "Islamic" so that "Europe" could better define itself as "Enlightened." What suffered was the organically worldly disposition of Islam, the fact that it was a definitively worldly religion, whose otherworldly perils and promises were entirely contingent on its historical experiences here and now.

It is crucial to recognize that the total Islamicity of the "Islamic societies" is an essentially ideological proposition, and unless we undo that proposed construction, we cannot unearth and retrieve the momentous tensions of theocentricity and anthropocentricity constitutional to any confrontation between the sacred and the worldly imaginations. One crucial consequence of this concealment was evident in the course of colonial encounters with European modernity when all potentially triumphant occasions of the cosmopolitan worldliness were categorically related to the realm of so-called Westernization with its magical reliance on the greatest myth of European modernity, "the West" itself—thus depriving Muslims of the terms of their own worldly emancipation at crucial historic conjunctions.

Let us consider the simple fact that there are more books, essays, and articles in English, French, German, and Italian with the apocryphal "Islam" and "Islamic" in their titles than there are in Arabic, Persian,

DOI: 10.1057/9781137301291

Turkish, or Urdu. Very rarely does the term "Islamic" appear in the entire spectrum of pre-modern Arabic, Persian, or Turkish primary sources. The term "Islamic" in fact begins to appear with some degree of frequency in modern Arabic, Persian, Turkish, or Urdu only after the Orientalist project had made it hegemonically viable. The colonial power of the French and the British was translated into the positivist power of the Orientalists to brand the object of their study "Islamic." The missionary zeal of the Christian Orientalists in particular was very conveniently attracted to the clerical institutions and sacred texts. Equally attracted to these texts were Orientalists, with the European project of Enlightenment as their sub-textual motivation. This dual attraction to "Islamic societies" is perhaps the only way that one can account for the overwhelming number of texts edited and translated by Orientalists in religious sciences, whereas the humanist sources (as one specific manifestation of the worldly) did not receive nearly as much attention in critical editions. The point here is not to distinguish the "religious" from the "humanist," but to point to their dialectical organicity in the intellectual history of Muslims.

Capitalized "Islam" was represented, made hegemonically possible, by and through the grand Orientalist project. Thus any hermeneutic of post-Orientalism must necessarily abandon all illusions of the determinacy of "Islam" and begin to reread historical communities in which the varieties of Qur'anic memories have, among many other forces, played a major role in the making of a cosmopolitan disposition. In this necessary act of rereading cultural history, texts and events must be read not in terms of their approximation to an absolutist/representationalist conception of "Islam" as a master-truth, but as the scattered testimony of moments of anxiety wherein the historical person has tried to cope with reality, or more accurately, with what Hans Blumenberg calls "the absolutism of reality," the sheer, unrelenting presence of being that ruthlessly demands an explanation, a placement. That placement has always been effectively worldly, in which Muslims have also appealed to their otherworldly sanctities. The organicity of that dialectic is what is lost in the Orientalist project, and in turn, in the Muslim responses to Orientalism.

The defiant imagination

Any understanding of the sources and sites of worldly imagination in confrontation or dialogue with the theocentricity of the Qur'anic, or

DOI: 10.1057/9781137301291

indeed the entire so-called Abrahamic memories, must be understood in its counter-positional anthropocentricity. To the degree that the Qur'anic imagination is irreducibly theocentric, the worldly imagination that came to fruition in its neighborhood and proximity was anthropocentric. Although the birth of "Man" as an historical person does not occur until much later in the history of these, as indeed many other, societies, a worldly conception of humanity (*al-Insan*) did exist to balance the omnipotent presence of the Qur'anic "God" (*Allah*). By "worldly imagination" I thus mean any act of creative imagination—be it narrative historiography or palace or mosque architecture—in which there is a detectable anthropocentricity in conscious or subconscious contradistinction to the theocentricity of the sacred. The centrality of the Qur'anic revelation in the Islamic sacred imagination should also function as the *contrapuntal* acid test of the worldly imagination. The creative imagination that casts the historic minutiae of being-in-the-world against the spectrum of the Qur'anic metanarrative must be, I contend, identified as "worldly." The Orientalist project (aided and abetted by Muslims responding to colonialism) robbed the assumption "Islamic" of that historic dialectic. I propose one makes no sense without the other—that the sacred has always had a worldly disposition, and the worldly a sacerdotal self-referentiality. The notion of "the secular" distorts that organicity and offers nothing instead.

In one particular manifestation of the worldly imagination, the art, we have the classical statement of Max Weber that can very well function as the first step in the construction of my argument here. "Just as ethical religion, ... " Weber observed, "enters into deepest inner tensions with the strongest irrational power of personal life, namely sexuality, so also does ethical religion enter into a strong polarity with the sphere of art."[10] It is in all acts of the aesthetic that we should look for the operation of the worldly imagination, even, or particularly, when it embraces the sacred. As Weber noted, the sacred imagination takes full advantage of the mobilizing and legitimizing powers of art in order to extend its aesthetic powers into the material domains of faith. In Islam the sacred and the worldly become inseparable—particularly in any act of the aesthetic—from mosque architecture to Qur'anic calligraphy. Weber notes:

> Religion and art are intimately related in the beginning. That religion has been an inexhaustible spring of artistic expressions is evident from the existence of idols and icons of every variety, and from the existence of music as a device for arousing ecstasy or for accompanying exorcism and apotropaic cultic actions. Religion has stimulated the artistic activities of

DOI: 10.1057/9781137301291

magicians and sacred bards, as well as stimulating the creation of temples and churches (the greatest of artistic productions), together with the creation of religious artifacts and church vessels of all sorts, the chief objects of the arts and crafts.[11]

To Weber's list one might add the Islamic mosques, Arabic and Persian calligraphy, and mystical poetry as specific examples of the creative imagination at the full service of the sacred. But that relationship in Islam is not mechanical—it is entirely organic, the two sides of the proposition effectively inseparable.

That organic link—between the worldly and the sacred—has had a crucial effect on both the aestheticization of the sacred and the sanctification of the aesthetic. In "The Relevance of the Beautiful," Gadamer fully recognized the functional dimensions of the act of artistic creation for the sacred.

> We should consider the position that Christianity adopted toward the artistic tradition in which it found itself. The rejection of iconoclasm, a movement that had arisen in the Christian Church during the sixth and seventh centuries, was a decision of incalculable significance. For the Church then gave a new meaning to the visual language of art and later to the form of poetry and narrative. This provided art with a new form of legitimation. The decision was justified because only the new content of the Christian message was able to legitimate once again the traditional language of art. One of the crucial factors in the justification of art in the West was the Biblia Pauperum, a pictoral narration of the Bible designed for the poor, who could not read or knew no Latin and who consequently were unable to receive the Christian message with complete understanding.[12]

Gadamer's example of *Biblia Pauperum* is remarkably reminiscent of the fate of the Persian passion play, or *Ta'ziyeh*, which at least since the sixteenth century, but with roots and indications certainly much earlier than that, has functioned as the dramaturgical staging of Shi'i martyrology. Popular in small towns and villages, Ta'ziyeh passion plays reached the widest and most common denominator of the Shi'i community as the central drama of their faith. In Shi'i performances, the worldly and the sacred become categorically intertwined.

Overshadowing that organicity is the colonial introduction of the notion of "the secular" (or Christianity in disguise as Gil Anidjar has persuasively demonstrated),[13] with which also enters the bourgeois commercialization of art, and its decided hostility to the sacred. The task facing Muslims is not to retrieve *the sacred* and to posit it against

DOI: 10.1057/9781137301291

the secular—a project most favored by reactionary thinkers like Seyyed Hossein Nasr,[14] but, instead, to reimagine the sacred in the immediate vicinity of its current worldliness.

Notes

1   For a detailed discussion of the word "kharabat" in Persian and Arabic sources, see Ahmad Ali Raja'i Bokhara'i, *Farhang Ash'ar Hafez* (Tehran: Ilmi Publications, 1364/1985): 179–198.

2   See Hafez's *Divan*. Edited by Mohammad Ghazvini and Ghasem Ghani (Tehran: Zavvar, 1320/1941): 245.

3   I extensively argue this case in my *Post-Orientalism: Knowledge and Power in Time of Terror* (New Brunswick, NJ: Transactions, 2008).

4   As cited by David Spurr in *The Rhetoric of Empire: Colonial Discourse in Journalism, Travel Writing, and Imperial Administration* (Durham, NC: Duke University Press Books, March 12, 1993): 4.

5   Ibid.

6   See Gayatri Spivak, "Subaltern Studies: Deconstructing Historiography," in Ranajit Guha, (Ed.), *Subaltern Studies* IV (New Delhi: Oxford University Press, 1985): 330–363.

7   Gianni Vattimo, *The Adventure of Difference: Philosophy after Nietzsche and Heidegger* (Baltimore, MD: Johns Hopkins University, 1993): 5.

8   Richard Rorty, *Objectivity, Relativism, and Truth* (Cambridge: Cambridge University Press, 1991): 1.

9   Friedrich Nietzsche, *Beyond Good and Evil: Prelude to a Philosophy of Future*. Translated with commentary by Walter Kaufmann (New York: Random House, 1966): 2.

10   Max Weber, *The Sociology of Religion*. Translated by Ephraim Fischoff (Boston: Beacon Press, 1993): 242.

11   Ibid: 242–243.

12   Hans Georg Gadamer, *The Relevance of the Beautiful and Other Essays* (Cambridge: Cambridge University Press, 1987): 3–4.

13   See Gil Anidjar, "Secularism" (*Critical Inquiry* 33: Autumn 2006).

14   See S. H. Nasr, *Knowledge and the Sacred* (New York: State University of New York Press, 1989).

DOI: 10.1057/9781137301291

3

The Muslim Cosmopole

Abstract: *In Chapter 3, I argue that being a Muslim in a post-Western world requires a critical re-thinking of Islamic cosmopolitanism as Muslims lived it over many centuries, before there was this binary trap of "Islam and the West." An active recollection of what that cosmopolitanism entailed enables the possibilities of inhabiting the renewed worldliness of Muslim lived experiences. The form of the thinking about Islam and of being a Muslim in the world will not be abstracted from this condition unless Muslims are located in the particularity of the end of that condition of post-coloniality.*

Dabashi, Hamid. *Being a Muslim in the World.* New York: Palgrave Macmillan, 2013. DOI: 10.1057/9781137301291.

DOI: 10.1057/9781137301291

My argument in the previous chapter was centered around the proposition that imagining ourselves in a post-Western world requires the dismantling of the regimes of knowledge with which the fiction of "the West" has historically sustained itself. I particularly targeted the binary between religion and secularism that I propose needs to be conceptually discarded in favor of a worldly conception of Islam that allows Muslims to be in their world and regenerate their collective consciousness with a full-bodied presence in their faith. In this chapter I wish to demonstrate how being a Muslim in a post-Western world requires a critical rethinking of Islamic cosmopolitanism as Muslims lived it over many centuries before the binary trap of "Islam and the West" camouflaged it. This active recollection of what that cosmopolitanism entailed will enable the possibilities of inhabiting the renewed worldliness of Muslims' lived experiences.

Adab: retrieving the literary

To remember the cosmopolitan worldliness of Muslims before their encounter with European colonial modernity there is no better place to start than with their vast and variegated field of *Adab*, or literary humanism.

Perhaps the single most powerful institution of literary imagination in Arabic—and by extension Persian, Turkish, and Urdu—has been that of Adab humanism. Although the institution of Adab, as George Makdisi has successfully demonstrated, is as old as the oldest legal institutions in Islam, the Orientalist imagination made it tangential to a dominant conception of "Islam" that Muslim clerics and non-clerical legal scholars perpetuate today. The Christian predilection of Orientalism as a totalizing project is perhaps at the root of this massive over-"juridicalization" of the Muslim worlds in a decidedly legalistic direction. But the full accounting of why the Orientalists were so adamant in this insistence requires much more detailed social and psychological acts of deconstruction, which at this stage of the task we face, would be rather useless.

In the totalizing act of Orientalism, juridical Islam, in a very vague, general, and panoramic view, was given the overriding power of defining just about everything in societies east of the Mediterranean. As late as 1968, when Frank Peters published his *Aristotle and the Arabs: The Aristotelian Tradition in Islam*, scarcely any trace of non-juridical, non-theological, or even non-philosophical sensibilities can be found in societies and cultures under the Orientalists' examination. To the by-then

DOI: 10.1057/9781137301291

established and classical story that the Arabs took their philosophizing enterprise exclusively from the Greeks and then introduced certain inconsequential twists into it, Peters adds a subplot: a constitutional lack of a humanist tradition among the Arabs. Let me quote Peters:

> The Western Hellenic trunk line whose way stations read: Ennius, Vergil, Horace, Quintilian, Cassiodorus, Alcuin, John of Salisbury, Dante, Petrarch, Scaliger, Bentley, Jowett, and Jebb has an Eastern counterpart, a shorter line to be sure, and bearing less traffic, but not without its interesting stops: Clement, Origen, Basil, Nemesius, John Philoponus, Sergius of Rish'ayna, Ibn al-Bitriq, al-Kindi, Hunayn ibn Ishaq, al-Farabi, Ibn Sina, Ibn Rushd. Behind the obvious exoticisms of language the two lists are quite different. The Western series is composed of humanists; the Eastern knows only philosophers and theologians. Names could be added to either, but the truth of each series remains. Western Hellenism is a variegated inheritance: philosophy, law, science, with a heavy insistence upon the humanities; humanitas, indeed, is a Roman word. Eastern Hellenism is constructed upon a much narrower base; its pillars are mathematics, geography, medicine, and philosophy; supporting them are Euclid, Ptolemy, Galen, and Aristotle. But for all this the East knows now Homer or Sophocles, and its Thucydides is a graceless Arab chronicler whose felicity is to collect endless chains of shaykhish transmitters.[1]

All other matters aside, the towering assumptions of this passage are the primacy of the Hellenist tradition in "giving" other people either an Aristotle or a Homer, that other people are not capable of producing their own philosophers and humanists, and that how much the poorer "the Eastern Hellenism" is for having borrowed one but not the other. The narrative plot is so high-handed and imperial that any attempt to point to the monumental bodies of Arabic odes or Persian epics would ultimately serve the recognition that the Arabs and Persians did borrow Homer after all.

Leaving the operative field of Orientalism proper, however, one need not look far or in obscure places to find strong, even thematic and persistent, literary tendencies in the Muslims' worldly imagination in their pre-colonial societies. The range of literary disciplines and institutions identified in the pioneering work of George Makdisi as "Adab-humanism" is by far the most prominent feature of medieval Muslim culture.[2] As F. Gabrieli has poignantly suggested, "the history of this word [Adab] reflects, parallel to and even better than the history of the words *Ilm* and *Din* [words representing Islamic jurisprudence and the

DOI: 10.1057/9781137301291

designation of the faith itself, respectively], the evolution of Arab culture from its pre-Islamic origins to our own day."[3]

From original references to good practical habits, social grace, public decorum, and so on, the term *Adab* gradually began to designate a vast literary institution in which nothing short of a worldly, liberal education was indispensable to an urbane, civilized life. Gabrieli has suggested that Adab be considered the functional equivalent of the Latin *urbanitas*, "the civility, courtesy, refinement of the cities."[4] As early as the seventh century, *Adab* explicitly suggested "the sum of knowledge that makes a man courteous and "urbane," profane culture (as distinct from *Ilm*, "learning," or rather, "religious learning," *Kur'an, Hadith,* and *fikh*) based in the first place on poetry, the art of oratory, and the historical and tribal traditions of the ancient Arabs, and also on the corresponding sciences: rhetoric, grammar, lexicography, metrics."[5] In and of itself, *Adab* was an institution.

As George Makdisi has fully documented it, the fertile field of humanism, quite independent of such figments of imaginative geography as "Western Hellenism" or "Eastern Hellenism," was evident in the seventh century, and fully established by the middle of the eighth. Khalaf al-Alhamar (d. 796), for example, in his *Muqaddimah fi al-Nahw* ("Prolegomena to Grammar") links the study of grammar directly to the arts of poetry and rhetoric and collectively represents them as institutionalized forms of learning.[6] The two great humanists, Abu 'Ubayda and al-Asma'i, who flourished during the reign of Harun al-Rashid, gave full textual evidence of the rising status of Adab humanism. Another great humanist, al-Mubarrad (d. 898), who came about a century after al-Asma'i and Abu Ubaydah, composed his magnum opus *al-Kamil* fully conscious that he was writing an encyclopedic manual of style for students of Adab consisting of "artistic prose, poetry, apophthegms, sermons, speeches, and letters."[7] Lest one confuse the significance given to grammar in Adab literature in nineteenth-century philological scientism, one must consider the remarks of Ibn Mammati (d. 1209), a humanist of Coptic Christian descent, who ridiculed those grammarians who did not study rhetoric, poetics, history, and narratology in conjunction with grammar. "The case of those grammarians," he observed, "is like that of the manufacturer of scales, who has nothing to weigh. Others acquire them and use them to weigh priceless pearls, precious gems, gold dinars and silver jewels."[8] The institution of Adab was no less exacting than any other field of superior learning.

DOI: 10.1057/9781137301291

In various classical sources on division of knowledge from this period, the entire spectrum of human understanding is divided into tree branches: (1) the literary arts, (2) the religious sciences, and (3) the "foreign sciences." Ahmad Ibn Yusuf Katib al-Khwarazmi in his *Mafatih al-'Ulum* (composed between 977 and 982) classified such Adab subjects as poetry and history side-by-side with patently doctrinal sciences as jurisprudence and theology, while he delegated the "foreign sciences" separately to his second chapter, where he categorizes philosophy, logic, medicine, and so on. Makdisi in fact alerts us that

> such a division does not show that the literary arts were propaedeutic to the foreign as well as to the Islamic sciences. But besides being ancillary to the two other divisions, the literary arts constituted a division of knowledge in themselves; an independent field in which students could pursue advanced studies, on a graduate level, as in the case of the other two divisions; like them, its professors had their fellows (ashab, pl. of sahib) who graduated under their direction. This independent field, called adab, was that of humanistic studies.[9]

When Ibn an-Nadim (d. 990) wrote his famous *al-Fihrist,* he followed the same tripartite division of knowledge in his ten chapters but gave noticeable primacy to humanist branches of knowledge, such as history and poetry, over dogmatic ones, such as jurisprudence and theology, followed by such branches of "foreign sciences" as philosophy.[10] Coming before both Ibn al-Nadim and al-Khwarazmi, al-Farabi (873–950) demonstrated his preference for both literary and philosophical knowledge by putting them both before the juridical sciences in his famous division of sciences called *Ihsa' al-'Ulum.* It is equally important to note that al-Farabi did not even categorize dogmatic sciences such as jurisprudence and theology independently and included them under the same chapter heading as social philosophy.[11] By the early part of the thirteenth century, the primacy and significance of literary studies had become so independent of both dogmatic and "foreign sciences" that Muhammad ibn Ali al-Sakaki (d. 1228) devoted his entire *Miftah al-'Ulum* to literary branches of knowledge and not a word is mentioned here of either juridical or the so-called foreign sciences.[12]

Arabic and Persian literary humanism must be considered the crowning achievement of what we might call Muslims' worldly imagination. Although the rise of humanism in Arabic has been traced back to "concern for…the sacred scripture" or "because of deep concern for the purity of the classical Arabic of the Koran as the living language,"[13] the fact remains that certainly by the eighth and ninth centuries, the

DOI: 10.1057/9781137301291

institution of Adab had assumed an autonomous status sui generis. The proposition that Arabic literary humanism came to fruition out of "deep concern for...the purity of the classical Arabic of the Koran" becomes less plausible if we consider the simultaneous formation of literary humanism in Persian, which as a non-canonical language, a language in which no sacred text was revealed, gave rise to a monumental body of worldly iterature to which diverse historical communities in Eastern Muslim empires contributed.

Even Makdisi, who postulates a concern for "the purity of the classical Arabic of the Koran" as the occasion of the rise of Arabic literary humanism, concedes that both humanism and its scholastic counterpart scholasticism had a distinct raison d'être "distinct from the other" and asserts that "both movements aimed for orthodoxy: humanism, for "orthodoxy" in language; scholasticism, for orthodoxy in religion."[14] What Makdisi calls "orthodoxy in language" can effectively be translated as the primacy of the literary imagination in humanism that stood in sharp contrast to the doctrinal mandates operative in scholasticism.

The overwhelming evidence of the central significance of Arabic poetic imagination in pre-Islamic Arab culture forces us to modify considerably Makdisi's assertion that "both humanism and scholasticism had their roots in religion."[15] Although it is clear that Islamic scholasticism is unimaginable without the active unfolding of the Qur'anic memory in juridical and theological directions, it is not also true that Arabic literary humanism is equally dependent on the Qur'anic revelation. From its pre-Islamic origin into its Islamic periods, Arabic humanism was a morally and aesthetically organic universe of imagination rooted in Muslims' world lives. The rise of Persian humanism, again as a counter-example, could not have any connection whatsoever to Arabic as the sacred language of the Qur'an, while in many of its dimensions it was either religiously syncretic, agnostic, or even blatantly anti-dogmatic. This is not positing Persian literary humanism as "anti-Islamic" but as integral to Muslim worldly experiences that are not entirely reducible to doctrinal absolutes.

Whereas the rise of humanism experiences one of its major zeniths by the end of the seventh century, it is not until the tenth century that Islamic scholasticism came to full doctrinal fruition. It is a remarkable historical irony that the Christianized Europe receives Arabic humanism and Islamic scholasticism in reverse order and is exposed much sooner to the latter than to the former.[16] The painstaking documentation of Makdisi, connecting *studia humanitatis* of the Italian renaissance to *studia*

DOI: 10.1057/9781137301291

adabiya in Arabic, should leave no doubt as to the irreducibly humanist, that is, worldly, origin of this creative imagination.

In addition to the centrality of Arabic language in Adab humanism, it is crucial to remember that Persian became a non-canonical language that had even greater distance from the sacred language of the Qur'an. Modern Persian, that is, the Persian that developed after the Arab invasion of Iran, emerged as a language in which no sacred text was revealed. The sacred memories of Avestan and Pahlavi faded into the blatantly non-doctrinal Persian, which during the medieval history functioned as a remissive, occasionally even subversive, language in which impermissible thought could be expressed. In subsequent fabrications of Hadith, as well as in early syncretic revolutionary movements in the seventh and eighth centuries, there are visible signs of attempts to elevate Persian to the status of a sacred language. The prophet was purported to have said that the people of Paradise spoke Persian. Such revolutionary leaders as Bihafarid in the eighth century were reported to have brought a new revelation in Persian. Later such monuments of Persian mystical poetry as Rumi's *Mathnavi* were praised as "the Qur'an in Persian." These were all rather nervous, but ultimately rhetorical, attempts to sanctify Persian from its subversive position vis-à-vis the sacred language of the Qur'an.

Muslim urban intellectuals

Whereas the politically powerful jurisconsults were financially secure because of the endowment arrangements of the *madrasah* system, the humanists were (by and large) part of the courtly apparatus. Makdisi reports that humanists were mostly "self-made men, whose fortunes varied from rags to riches, and back again. But they were not without help. Books began to appear with humanists particularly in mind.... They searched for manuscripts, bought or copied them, collected libraries. Books were written, with autodidacts in mind, on the divisions and classifications of knowledge, on the technical terminology of various fields of learning."[17] This group of urban literati soon began to be identified in biographical dictionaries as *Ahl al-Adab* (the humanists). The humanists were as conscious of themselves as others were of them. Tawhidi reports that Ali b. Jahm (d. 863) was heard singing the praises of the great poet Abu Tammam, inspiring someone to remark that had the poet been Ali's brother he could hardly have praised him more. Ali answered that

DOI: 10.1057/9781137301291

although the poet was not his brother through family kinship, he was his brother through the kinship of humanism. He then quoted three verses the poet had addressed to him, of which this was the final hemistich: "[A]dab to which we have given the position of progenitor."[18]

The principal exponents of literary humanism were themselves fully conscious of their status as a distinct group of urban intellectuals with highly cultivated tastes for literary arts. In *Irshad al-Arib ila Ma'rifah al-Adib*, Yaqut, having given lip service to the "otherworldly" benefits of scholastic studies, with lavish praise shows his love for humanism:

> [Humanism is not] *of the variety that has a ready market in the madrasa-colleges, or that one can use in scholastic disputations in ceremonial gatherings. Rather, it is the learning of kings and prime ministers, of people of eminence and masters, who make it a springtime meadow for their hearts, a pleasurable entertainment for their minds, a relaxing recreation for their souls, and on which their joys shower their blessings. For this learning is the springtime of excellent minds, and the cost price of the superior sciences.*[19]

Makdisi rightly notes that "having paid his respects to religions, Yaqut could now afford to give voice to his true thoughts as to humanism's place vis-à-vis its rival in religious studies; namely, law and the scholastic method, and all the fanfare and fracas of its obstreperous refinement."[20] Makdisi then reveals his own true thoughts on humanism:

> Adab moves in an atmosphere of grandeur and urbane elegance. Its world is that of kings and prime ministers, chancellors and high functionaries, adepts and lovers of the language arts, held in the high honor in the royal courts, where wit and repartee, elegance of dress and eloquence of speech are the coin of the realm. In reading this work of Yaqut, replete with the record of humanistic activity in Islamic history up to his time, the reader can hardly miss his message.[21]

In view of these and many similar passages in which Makdisi fully documents the institutional autonomy of Adab humanism, it is rather curious that he is reluctant to admit its active operation as a patently non-canonical, self-consciously worldly institution. At one point he observes:

> The ties between adab studies and religious studies in Islam being as close as they were, it was almost a contradiction in terms to speak of secularist humanism. There was never a break between humanism and religion.[22]

But these are two different issues, which the great scholar of Arab humanism confuses. Adab was organic to the mind of a Muslim intellectual, and

DOI: 10.1057/9781137301291

thus not "secular"; but neither was it "religious." Makdisi feels obligated, however, to modify his position by adding, "that is not to say, however, that, at least with some humanists, a more or less deep exposure to the writings of Greece, India, and Persia, three ancient cultures that had their influence on adab, did not tend to encourage a skeptical attitude which went to the point of heresy, albeit of infrequent occurrence."[23] As worldly intellectuals, the Muslim literati were of course never disrespectful but in fact were perfectly tolerant of people's sacrosanct sentiments. The humanists were a self-conscious group of urban literati fully cognizant of the open-minded liberality of their aesthetic imagination. "There was a consciousness among humanists that they formed a class apart in society."[24] We also know that "if a humanist had thoughts of a critical or skeptical nature towards religion, he did well to keep them to himself."[25] The question is not whether particular humanists were "religious or secular"—two entirely anachronistic terms for them. The issue is the historical and institutional presence and legitimacy of a worldly mode of imagination with monumental literary output to sustain and support it. Within the literary space thus crafted there existed the historical possibility of a non-sacred, patently worldly, encounter with being. One cannot subject individual humanists to transhistorical (and above all anchoretic) psychoanalysis to determine who was "a religious and who a secular" thinker. What is clear is that the magnificent body of humanist literature, prose and poetry, could not have been produced in the spare time of otherwise doctrinaire clerics. These urban literati were integral to a cosmopolitan worldliness in which "Islam" was floating without needing to name itself.

Multicultural humanism

From an originally limited, Arabic-based humanism, the institution of Adab eventually grew, in the late Umayyad–early Abbasid period, into a multicultural phenomenon of unsurpassed significance. The expansion of the empire gave rise to a specific kind of urban intellectual, comfortable and conversant in a number of cultural traditions. A multicultural exposure to Arab, Iranian, Indian, and even Chinese and Greek traditions became a staple of Adab humanism.

> The adib of the 3rd/9th century, of which al-Djahiz was the most perfect example, was therefore not only cultivated in Arabic poetry and prose, in

DOI: 10.1057/9781137301291

maxims and proverbs, in the genealogy and tradition of the djahiliyyah and of the Arabs at a time when they were hardly yet Islamicized, but broadened out his range of interest to include the Iranian world with all its epic, gnomic, and narrative tradition, the Indian world with its fables, and the Greek world with its practical philosophy, and especially its ethics and economics. It was thus that in the 3rd/9th century there came into being the great literature of Adab, with its varied and pleasing erudition, which is not pure scholarship although it often also touches on, and handles scientific subjects, but which is centered above all on man, his qualities and his passions, the environment in which he lives, and the material and spiritual culture created by him.[26]

A humanist's descent from a non-Islamic tradition was of no consequence whatsoever. Ibn Mammati (d. 1209), a statesman-humanist under the Ayyubid, was of Coptic Christian decent.[27] Abu Ubaydah Ma'mar ibn al-Muthanna', a leading humanist during the reign of Harun al-Rashid, was of Jewish-Persian origins.[28] Ibn al-Muqaffa', a legendary stylist and translator of literary works from Pahlavi and Sanskrit into Arabic, was of Zoroastrian-Persian extraction. Ibn Abd Rabbihi of Cordova, the author of the greatly influential text in humanist learning, *al-Iqd al-Farid*, was descended from a slave of the Spanish Umayyad caliph, Hisham ibn Abd al-Rahman (reigned 788–796). Abu al-Faraj al-Isfahani (898–968), the very model of a literary humanist and author of the monumental work *al-Aghani*, a compendium of pre-Islamic Arab songs, was a descendant of the Quraysh tribe, born and raised in Isfahan, came to fruition in Baghdad, and was patronized handsomely by the Persian Buwayhid vizier, al-Muhallabi (d. 963). As Makdisi has noted:

> It is true that the fields of Adab themselves were considered "neutral," so to speak, as far as religion was concerned. For whereas, in order to study the Islamic religious sciences one had to be a Muslim, the humanistic studies were open to non-Muslims. These studies were available outside of the mosque and other institutions of learning based on the charitable trust, waqf. Such was the case of the non-Muslim historian, Hilal as-Sabi (d. 448/1056), who is said to have "studied under the [Muslim] scholars, while an infidel," this anomaly being explained as follows: "because he was pursuing adab studies" …. The neutrality of the studia adabiya, in this regard, explains the existence of Christians, Jews and Sabians, not only in "foreign sciences," such as medicine and astronomy, but also in the studia adabiya.[29]

What Makdisi terms "neutral" is in effect a self-consciously non-canonical discourse institutionalized in the historical foregrounding of Adab

DOI: 10.1057/9781137301291

humanism. What mattered was the cosmopolitan literacy of a group of urban intellectuals in conscious association with each other, irrespective of any other aspect of their communal identity. "Within this domain," Gabrieli has suggested, "al-Djahiz and his followers (Abu Hayyan al-Tawhidi, al-Tanukhi, etc.) turn to account and extended the heritage bequeathed to Muslim society in the previous century by the Iranian genius Ibn al-Mukaffa', who can be described as the true creator of this enlarged conception of adab, with his versions of foreign historical and literary works (Khuday-namak and Kalilah wa-Dimna) and his original ethical and didactic tracts (*al-Adab al-Kabir* and *al-Saghir*).[30] That a Persian of Zoroastrian origin became the defining moment of Arabic Adab humanism, in and of itself, is sufficient to suggest the polyvocal origin of Muslim worldly consciousness.

The Shu'ubiyyah movement

Nowhere is the cosmopolitan construction of Adab humanism more evident than in the Shu'ubiyyah movement of the eighth and ninth centuries. As Hamilton Gibb put it, the Shu'ubiyyah movement "was not a mere conflict between two schools of literature, nor yet a conflict of political nationalism, but a struggle to determine the destinies of the Islamic culture as a whole."[31] If the implications of the Shu'ubiyyah as a movement were indeed taken seriously, the canonical assumption of the term "Islamic societies" would have to be radically reconsidered. The Shu'ubiyyah represented an active urbanization of an expansionist military culture that had brought together the social and economic forces of a number of major civilizations immediately preceding it. It was not just "Arabs" and "Persians," as the assumptions of two ethnic abstractions, but also urban communities formed of a multitude of groups, classes, and social strata that came together to form a sedentary culture in dire need of all the civilizing forces of a post-charismatic period. The explosion of the Muhammadan charismatic movement had broken through the classical patrimonialism of the tribal society and mobilized its energies in establishing the initial "Muslim" community.[32]

During Muhammad's career as a revolutionary prophet (610–632), he transformed the scattered energies of Arab patrimonialism into a concentrated energy for articulating his vision of the new *ummah*. In the immediate aftermath of the Prophet's death, the period of the "Rightly-Guided

DOI: 10.1057/9781137301291

Caliphs" (632–661), that patrimonialism successfully wedded itself to the emerging "Islamic" vision and reinvented itself in the form of the Umayyad dynasty (661–750). But the Umayyad dynasty paradoxically dug an ever-deeper grave for its own tribal patrimonialism with every new conquest into the Byzantine and Sassanid empires. The rise to power of the Abbasids (750–1258) signaled the triumph of the urban elite's new cosmopolitan multiculturalism, which was squarely founded on the economic and social institutions necessitated by the Umayyad military expansions, over the tribal patrimonialism that had survived throughout the Umayyad period. The administrative, literary, and philosophical attraction to the Sassanid and Byzantine traditions thus coincided with the formation of a Veblenian "leisure class"[33] in Baghdad and other major cosmopolitan sites. The cultural by-products of an expanded and multi-"national" economy and polity made possible by the military expansionism of the early period, and emerging from the most formidable intellectual forces in the newly formed multicultural communities, the Shu'ubiyyah movement thus became the political aspiration of urban intellectuals hoping to define the new universal culture in aesthetic and literary terms rather than tribal and sectarian ones. It is not accidental that Adab humanism in general, and Arabic poetry in particular, became the breeding ground of the Shu'ubiyyah. Nor is it accidental that the combined forces of tribal patrimonialism and the juridical establishment reacted so violently to the Shu'ubiyyah movement.

In Hamilton Gibb's classical reading of the Shu'ubiyyah movement, despite the fact that he radically shifted the terms of analysis toward social and cultural developments, the binary opposition is still cast in Persian-Arab rivalries:

> The issue at stake was no superficial matter of literary modes and fashions, but the whole cultural orientation of the new Islamic society—whether it was to become a re-embodiment of the old Perso-Aramaean culture into which the Arabic and Islamic elements would be absorbed, or a culture in which the Perso-Aramaean contributions would be subordinated to Arab tradition and the Islamic values.[34]

Gibb's accurate depiction of bona fide cultural warfare is marred by his identification of it with "Arabs" and "Persians" (or, alternatively, "Perso-Aramaean," with Aramaean having been "heavily Persianized"). The evident warfare here is really not between "the Arabs" and "the Persians," but

DOI: 10.1057/9781137301291

between the tribal patrimonialism that was the basis of the Muhammadan prophetic movement and a rising cosmopolitan urbanism that included both Arabs and Persians, as well as many other *Mawali* groupings that did not necessarily fit those categorical imperatives. To be sure, there was an element of multicultural urbanism evident in the Sassanid Empire that was obviously lacking in pre-Islamic tribalism in Arabia. But the Abbasid Empire, over which presided caliphs of mostly Arab descent, had created an entirely unprecedented economic and political universe into which were poured Greek, Byzantine, Persian, (and later Turkish, Indian, and Central Asian) cultural forces. That economic and political universe corresponded to an energetic moral and intellectual imagination that urban intellectuals of the Shu'ubiyyah bent were not ready to abandon, either to a tribal patrimonialism or to a narrowly literalistic reading of the Muhammadan legacy. As an alternative, the Shu'ubis stood for a highly cultivated aesthetic urbanism that included the universal appeal of the Muhammadan legacy but was by no means reducible to its potential tribalism.

The magisterial presence of Ibn Muqaffa' (d. 757), born of Persian descent and risen to the highest achievements of Arabic literary humanism, in early Adab history, is perhaps the most eloquent example of the sort of urbanity championed by the Shu'ubiyyah movement. Before he was brutally tortured and murdered by Sufyan ibn Mu'awiyah, Ibn Muqaffa' personified the most brilliant promise of an urban intellectual, fully at home in a language and a literature not of his parents. Born in Firuzabad in Fars to Persian parents, Ibn Muqaffa became the paramount practitioner of Arabic prose, enriching it with such translations from Pahlavi as *Kalilah wa Dimnah* or *The Khuday-namak*. In such original Arabic compositions as *Kitab Adab al-Kabir* and *Risalah fi al-Sahabah*, Ibn Muqaffa' contributed not only to the transformation of Arabic language into a potent literary medium but also to the active formation of a moral imagination that in both politics and culture could sustain an entire civilization. Ibn Muqaffa' was a Manichean convert to Islam, though the degree of his "conversion" to the faith ought to be measured against the evidence of the Manichaean "Apologia" attributed to him (not to mention his *Mu'aradat al-Qur'an*, in which he is believed to have broken the greatest doctrinal taboo of the faith by "imitating" the sacred text). Beyond these perhaps more radical gestures, what matters is the rooted urbanity of the figure of the Muslim intellectual, for whom the cosmopole is the active universe of his creative imagination.

DOI: 10.1057/9781137301291

The poetic imagination

That creative imagination was multivariate. In both Arabic and Persian, the two leading languages of the eastern and western parts of the Abbasid empire and beyond and after, an active poetic imagination of the most varied, effervescent energy created and sustained an independent aesthetics irreducible to any sacred metanarrative, and not entirely hostile or even disrespectful of it. Squarely grounded on a rich and diversified pre-Islamic (*Jahiliyyah*) tradition, Arabic poetry defied the Qur'anic inhibition (26:224 ff.) and became the crowning achievement of medieval Adab humanism. Even purported Prophetic traditions, such as "[v]erily it would be better for a man to have his belly filled with pus until it destroys him than to fill himself with poetry," failed to prevent the phenomenal rise of Arabic and Persian (as well as Turkish and, later, Urdu) poetry of the most varied forms. Such great architects of medieval Arabic poetry as Abu Nuwas (d. circa 810) are considered "not surpassed in poetical genius by any ancient bard."[35] Abu Nuwas became the poetic personification of a flamboyant and jubilant rejection of tribal morality. Born to Persian parents in Ahwaz, Abu Nuwas became the most outspoken poetic voice of an urban humanism that defied both the tribal patrimonialism of the Umayyad/Abbasid patriarchy and the literalist legalism of the Ulama, and as such was definitive to Arabic poetic cosmopolitanism.

In another great medieval poet, Abu al-Atahiyah (748–828), we witness the active and oppositional formation of a poetic morality self-consciously irreducible to Qur'anic doctrines.[36] He was attracted to such alternative religious ideas as those of Manichaeism. But beyond anything else in the simplified poetic diction of his choice, he created a "moral" world in which one could live independently of any scholastic jurisprudence. Like many other great poets of his rank, Abu al-Atahiyah was perpetually in trouble with the political establishment, which was always over-anxious to demonstrate its legitimacy to the clerical establishment. In the case of al-Mutanabbi (915–965), his creation of an autonomous moral universe in his poetry went so far that he was followed as a prophet (thus the origin of his name). A remarkable friendship and camaraderie developed between him and his patron prince Sayf al-Dawlah that demonstrates the nature of the political culture that Adab humanism could generate and sustain.

When we come to a poet like Abu al-Ala' al-Ma'arri (973–1057) we realize the remarkable degree to which the poetic imagination in Arabic

DOI: 10.1057/9781137301291

could transgress the sacred and constitute an aesthetic domain at once operative and illuminative. Born and raised in Syria and blinded in childhood by smallpox, al-Ma'arri spent a year and a half in Baghdad, where the intellectual and artistic effervescence of that medieval capital of the civilized world cultivated his moral and critical imagination. In view of one critic, al-Ma'arri was "one of the greatest moralists of all time whose profound genius anticipated much that is commonly attributed to the so-called modern spirit of enlightenment."[37] The following quatrain neatly sums up what he thought of clerical scholasticism:

> Hanifs are stumbling, Christian all astray,
> Jews wildered, Magians far on error's way.
> We mortals are composed of two great schools—
> Enlightened knaves or else religious fools.[38]

Lest we think these the private whisperings of a lonely poet, we need only read the remarkable account by Naser Khosrow, the great Persian Isma'ili poet, philosopher, and traveler who, as historical fate would have it, visited al-Ma'arri's\'s birthplace when he was still alive and reports:

> *In that city [Ma'arra] was a man known as Abu al-'Ala al-Ma'arri. He was blind, and yet he was the chief (ra'is) of the city. He was abundantly rich and had many servants and agents. The inhabitants of the city in their entirety were devoted to him. But he himself was an ascetic man. He was modestly clothed, remaining secluded in his home, and having nothing but a piece of barley bread for sustenance. I heard that the doors to his house were always open, and that his representatives and agents attended to the matters of the city and did not consult with him except in general terms. He did not deny anyone from his abundant wealth. As for himself, he led an extremely pious and ascetic life, refusing to have anything to do with worldly matters. And yet this man has such a profound status in poetry and adab that the most learned in Sham [Syria], Maghrib [North Africa], and Iraq [Mesopotamia] consider him the best who has ever been....Someone once asked him, "God Almighty has given you so much wealth in abundance. Why is it that you give it all away and do not enjoy it yourself?" He responded, "Nothing more than I eat belongs to me." When I reached there, this man was still alive.*[39]

Rich and powerful as the poetic imagination was in the Arabic language, it was even more so once the Persian language became equally fertile with its creative force in the eastern part of the Muslim world. The very formation of Persian as a literary and poetic medium, out of a fruitful transformation of Pahlavi, constituted a formidable space wherein

DOI: 10.1057/9781137301291

forbidden thoughts could be expressed. By the time of Rudaki (d. circa 940), Persian poets had already established a literary aesthetics constitutional to their emerging cosmopolitanism.

The composition of Ferdowsi's *Shahnameh* in about the year 1009 provides the most magnificent evidence of a Persian poetic imagination that was self-consciously self-referential in the authority of its aesthetics. More than anything else, Ferdowsi's *Shahnameh* is evidence of a narrative autonomy in Persian poetic imagination irreducible to anything from the Islamic scholasticism. Though he was a Muslim (and evidently a Shi'i), Ferdowsi composed *Shahnameh* from the oral and written sources of pre-Islamic epic narratives. From its non-canonical Persian language to its pre-Islamic Iranian sources, epic narrative, and, ultimately, autonomous poetic composition, the *Shahnameh* is solid, enduring evidence of a mode of cultural presence entirely irrelevant to Islamic scholasticism, and of a Muslim cosmopolitan worldliness irreducible to doctrinal dogmas.

Two crucial aspects of the *Shahnameh* center it in a mode of cultural presence almost entirely poetic and non-metaphysical. First and foremost is its manifestation of the Persian poetic arts; second are its passionate acts of storytelling. Most literary historians agree that Ferdowsi's epic constitutes the zenith of Persian poetic arts,[40] in which Ferdowsi employs the highest achievements of the preceding generation of poetic dictions to narrate one of its most aesthetically wholesome works of art. As a result, the text constitutes an event in Persian poetic consciousness, following which one can safely argue that there is a cultural mode of being that is in an identifiable sense aesthetic rather than metaphysical. The *Shahnameh* is predicated on no sacred assumption, grounded on no metaphysics, and rests on nothing but the sheer power of words conjuring up worlds within and beyond themselves. A dramatic, romantic, poetic narrative with an unrivaled power to enchant, *Shahnameh* has for generations held an entire people spellbound, richly sustaining their moral and political imaginations beyond metaphysical reach. Ferdowsi was a Muslim, to be sure, but his *Shahnameh* was not the product of an Islamic sacred universe—it is precisely that factual organicity that needs to be understood and conceptually retrieved today.

The passionate art of storytelling so abundantly evident in the *Shahnameh* points to yet another dimension of the enduring power of this work. Whether painted, read, or recited, these stories have made generations of Afghans, Iranians, or Tajiks (practicing Muslims though they may be) aware of a poetic presence entirely *sui generis*. These

DOI: 10.1057/9781137301291

stories constitute an historical consciousness, a cultural self-awareness, a political cognizance at once moral and poetic, normative and aesthetic, with equal claims to being "true" and beautiful. The folkloric adaptation of *Shahnameh* as an epic in the remotest corners of Iranian culture have saved the text from becoming a mere artifact at the service of the Persian monarchy. Through lucrative commissions of magnificent *Shahnameh* paintings, the Persian monarchy has sought to appropriate the text into the apparatus of its legitimacy; the work has had, however, far-reaching implications beyond such controls. The open-ended and multisignificatory nature and function of the *Shahnameh* stories are the very staple of a mode of cultural memory that in its non-canonicity accommodates a poetic, constitutionally counter-metaphysical, mode of being.

The translation of *Shahnameh* into Arabic by al-Bundari in 1223–1224 and even before that the composition of *Ghurar Akhbar Muluk al-Furs wa Siaruhum* by al-Tha'alibi (d. 1037) point to the fact that Ferdowsi's epic had a literary and poetic reach far beyond the Persian-speaking world.

Visions of an aesthetic imagination

The varied and multiple domains of Muslim cosmopolitanism can be extended far beyond Adab humanism into related and/or adjacent fields. What has been categorically called the "Islamic art" conceals a phenomenal aesthetic force by no means limited in its creative effervescence to the particular mandates of the Qur'anic metanarrative. The supposition that if "a person with a modicum of artistic culture leaf[s] through photographs of major works of art from the world over...almost automatically a group of works would be identifiable as Islamic, Muslim, Moorish, Muhammadan, or Saracenic, because they shared a number of commonly known features"[41] may indeed point to certain common aesthetic sensibilities in this art, but by no means do we need to take the Orientalist proclivity for othering (by labeling art Islamic, Muslim, Moorish, Muhammadan, or Saracenic) at face value. An overwhelming number of local and a number of universal features unite, as much as separate Persian miniatures from Turkish and Indian ones, or the architecture of the Safavid Iran from that of the Ottomans or the Mughals. As Grabar points out, "Islamic" does not refer to the art of a particular religion, for a vast proportion of the monuments have little if anything to do with the faith of Islam."[42]

DOI: 10.1057/9781137301291

If that be the case, and "Islamic" here does not mean "Islamic," then the question is why call it "Islamic"? If indeed "there is... a Jewish Islamic art, since large Jewish communities lived within the predominantly Muslim world, and representative examples of this Jewish art have been included in a book on Arab painting," and if indeed "there is also a Christian Islamic art, most easily illustrated by metalwork from the Fertile Crescent in the thirteenth century but known elsewhere as well," and, ultimately, if "there is an Islamic art of India which was certainly not entirely an art of Muslims,"[43] then is it not more logical to conclude that "Islamic art," as Orientalist scholarship has defined it, is essentially a misnomer, that it, and other such generic terms as Muslim, Moorish, Muhammadan, or Saracenic, are othering terms constitutional to the Orientalist project of concocting a shadow for "the West"? Since "the West" itself was the most enchanting tale of all in the European project of Enlightenment modernity, "the Islamic," as indeed "the Oriental," became an epithet for creating and alienating an essential other that would sustain and legitimize its counterpart. Otherwise, when we read a distinguished historian of "Islamic art" like the late Oleg Grabar, who wrote that "the important point is that 'Islamic' in the expression 'Islamic art' is not comparable to 'Christian' or 'Buddhist' in 'Christian art' or 'Buddhist art,'"[44] we may think we are in a twilight zone where things do not mean what they say and yet continue to demand our credulity. If artists and architects of Muslim, Jewish, Christian, or Hindu faith produce paintings or buildings that shares certain features, would it not be more logical to attribute this to a material and aesthetic universe that transcends their sacred identity without negating it? If indeed such constructions as "Jewish Islamic art" or "Christian Islamic art" or "Indian Islamic art" can be plausible, then "Islamic art" refers to an organicity of the sacred and the worldly that is unique unto itself and cannot be divided into the religious and the secular—and it is that organicity that I call "worldly." Otherwise, what would remain of "Islam," and what could it mean if it were twisted and turned to be as much Jewish as Christian, as much Christian as Hindu?

The supposition that the term "Islamic" in fact "refers to a culture or civilization in which the majority of the population or at least the ruling element profess the faith of Islam"[45] is not convincing either, because it is the nature and disposition of that "culture" that are at issue here. By privileging the term "Islamic culture" we have already decided on a notion of the Islamicity of that culture that categorically disfigures such non-scholastic (non-juridical, non-canonical) elements as those evident

DOI: 10.1057/9781137301291

in the aesthetic imagination that, ipso facto, point to directions beyond, and indeed prohibited by, the letter of the law and the mandates of jurists. It is precisely this legalistic disposition of "Islam," as Orientalists have manufactured it, that is at issue here.

There is no question that with the rise of the Abbasids to power in the mid-eighth century, we witness a phenomenal aesthetic effervescence in the art and architecture of areas under their direct rule. But the material circumstances occasioned by that empire, the fact that the Abbasids brought Indian, Chinese, central Asian, Turkish, Persian, Arab, and Greek traditions into close proximity to each other, goes a long way in explaining this development that the distortive factors embedded in the term "Islamic," as in "religious," could organically sustain. To be sure, the same material success created conditions conducive to the phenomenal advancement in Islamic scholasticism proper. Such specifically scholastic branches of knowledge as Qur'anic hermeneutics, Hadith scholarship, jurisprudence, and theology developed to highly complex degrees, thus constituting the legitimate institutionalization of the faith as a universal religion with a vast intellectual underpinning. But that is not tantamount to an assumption that the entire society or culture that was concurrent with this institutionalization of scholasticism was scholastic. That scholasticism in fact received much of its rhetorical power from fierce opposition to forces like those evident in the aesthetic imagination. The dialectical interface between *humanism* and *scholasticism* points to a cosmopolitan organicity that, prior to the fateful Muslim encounter with European imperialism, had a reality sui generis—the logic and rhetoric of which are definitive to our renewed understanding of Muslims cosmopolitanism.

A folkloric imagination

The notion of cosmopolitan worldliness I am proposing should not be solely affiliated with the royal courts and literary formalism—they belong to the Muslim world at large. The presence of an extensive "folkloric imagination" testifies to the effervescence of a popular creativity that by no stretch of imagination is reducible to scholastic juridicalism in doctrinal or even "cultural" terms. As a prominent example of the folkloric imagination one may refer to the collection of stories known to us as "The Arabian Nights," or "The Thousand and One Nights." Of diverse

DOI: 10.1057/9781137301291

Indian, Persian, and Arabic origins, "The Thousand and One Nights" is regarded as "the expression of the lay and secular imagination" against "the austere erudition and religious zeal" of its context.[46] If we take the text of "The Thousand and One Nights" out of its recent Orientalization for the exotic entertainment of its European translators and put it back in its local context, we can then indeed see it as a remarkable document in which a folkloric imagination subverts the dominant austerity of the official culture. While the original title of "The Thousand and One Nights," or, in its Persian origins, "Hazar Afsaneh,"[47] had a more symbolic reference to the number "one thousand and one," in its numerous renditions in Arabic and Persian, the number provided ample opportunity for creative additions by various communities.

Although various attempts must have been made to give them a singular narrative in print, it was not until well into the eighteenth century that a printed version began to dominate the oral tradition.[48] But both before and after their textualization, the stories of "The Thousand and One Nights" were essentially oral and folkloric in nature. The fact that scarcely any two manuscripts have precisely the same content points to the widespread folkloric reproductions of these stories in multiple contexts and cultures. While the European Orientalists adopted the text for their exoticization of their imaginary "Orient," some scholars of Arabic literature have denounced this version as sub-standard and "decadent."[49] But it is precisely its "fortuitous, wild, more or less rank growth, . . . its non-erudite character, its disparate contents, and the quality of the language it uses—never up to the standards of good 'literary' Arabic"[50] that sets "The Thousand and One Nights" apart as a flamboyant narrative carnival of enormous significance in the history and texture of a vast, worldly, and even mundane, imagination that forces our understanding of "Islamic societies" toward a greater cosmopolitan worldliness than the term suggests.

As crucial as "The Thousand and One Nights" is in its widespread representation of folkloric imagination, it is not the only record that has reached us. For an alternative example in the Persian context one may refer to the story "Samak Ayyar," which is equally representative of a rich and subversive folkloric imagination. Although the final rendition of this story has come to us from a certain Faramarz ibn Khodad ibn Abdollah al-Kateb al-Arjani, and though the author himself attributes his version (probably composed in late eleventh or early twelfth century) to a Sadaqeh ibn abi al-Qasim al-Shirazi, the story has roots further

DOI: 10.1057/9781137301291

in the past.[51] As a folkloric story, "Samak Ayyar" has been re-narrated generation after generation in a multitude of communities throughout the Persian-speaking world.

The adventures of Samak Ayyar are representatives of the entire typical category of "Ayyari" or "Javanmardi" or "fotovvat" in which measures of "manhood" were defined and tested in good deeds, which the powerful feared and the powerless hoped for. While the narrative structure of popular stories such as "Samak Ayyar" remains the same, their generational and local variations reveal their adaptations to specific historical communities.[52] Although a politically court-based and profoundly literary culture ultimately seeks to textualize and give a master narrative to stories such as "Samak Ayyar," they nevertheless contain profoundly folkloric and popular bases outside the purview of both the political and the clerical establishments. While the court and the mosque actively seek to monopolize the written memory of the culture and thus to control and guide it, the creative effervescence of folkloric imagination finds outlet in spaces outside of these two power-based environments. In its royal, military, epic, romantic, social, and cultural dispositions, "Samak Ayyar" reveals a broad-based and actively self-confident popular imagination. The crucial point in the story's moral composition is that it is not reducible to "Islam" in its Orientalist genealogy. *Ayyari*, or "chivalry," was a counter-moral disposition sui generis. In the various modes of "swearing" common among the Ayyars, "there is no sign of being a Muslim."[53] Of patently pre-Islamic, and in many instances old Iranian, nature, such expressions as *Yazdan-e Dadar* ("Mighty God"), *Asl-e Pakan va Nikan* ("the essence of the pure and the good"), or *Zand va Pazand* ("Holy Zoroastrian texts") obviously intend an archaic and non-Islamic moral disposition within the confinements of which the folkloric imagination operates.

The historical imagination

The presence of at least two great historians, Beyhaqi (circa 966–1077) and Ibn Khaldun (1332–1406), clearly demonstrates that there has been the creative force of an "historical imagination" in these so-called Islamic societies. What we see in them, chief among many other, is a clear and concise conception of history as a material reality in its own terms. These historians were obviously aware of the Qur'anic conceptions of time and narrative, this- and other-worldly divisions in human destiny,

DOI: 10.1057/9781137301291

and the fact that in the Qur'anic sacred subtext there is a Divinity that shapes our end, as it were. But such Qur'anic subtexts, constitutional to the institutionalization of Islam as a world religion, have no paramount place in Beyhaqi's or Ibn Khaldun's conceptions of history qua history. As Marilyn Waldman demonstrated in her pioneering study of Beyhaqi's *Ta'rikh*, this medieval Persian historian's use of narrative strategies reveals "a self-consciously innovative statement about how history should be done."[54] In Waldman's words:

> *Bayhaqi makes it easy for the reader to tell whether he is, in [Mary Louise] Pratt's words,[55] "not only reporting but also verbally displaying a state of affairs, inviting his addressee(s) to join him in contemplating it, evaluating it, and responding to it." Indeed, Bayhaqi tells his reader he is so doing at the end of almost every set of narratives and interpolations. His use of words that encourage interpretation abounds. His khutbah on history explicitly argues for telling "tellable" history. He constantly calls upon the reader to reflect, marvel, condemn. Implicitly as well, by his use of interpolation to comment on, and expand the meaning of, events, by his inclusion of human detail unnecessary to sheer informing, Bayhaqi displays a preoccupation with the relevance of tellability.[56]*

Thus considering Beyhaqi "in philosophical history and in criticism of sources foreshadow[ing] the more systematic contributions of Ibn Khaldun,"[57] Waldman demonstrates the remarkable narrative self-consciousness of the medieval historian. In the primacy of that narrative, history becomes a reality sui generis; telling it, a matter of literary-humanist art. Indeed as Waldman notes, "his work may also be a Persian counterpart of the development of 'Arab Humanism.'"[58] Although the historical formation of Persian Adab humanism is almost concomitant with that of Arab Adab humanism, in which Persians fully participated, it exceeds in its narrative varieties the historical diction represented by Beyhaqi, Waldman is accurate in her assessment of the literary significance of Beyhaqi's "History." What that history, in its self-conscious literary self-celebration, demonstrates is a full awareness of time and narrative as, in Ricoeur's terms, realities materially autonomous from any sacred appropriation of them into "Time Immemorial" and "Truth," the very staples of all biblical and Qur'anic metanarratives.

The same, in even stronger terms, is applicable to Ibn Khaldun who, as Muhsin Mahdi has demonstrated,[59] in effect systematized a whole *kulturewissenschaft* unprecedented in any institutionalized discourse traceable to either the Qur'anic memory or any other biblical metanarrative. Based on philosophical dispositions going back to Plato, Aristotle, Alfarabi,

Avicenna, al-Ghazali and, ultimately, Averroes, Ibn Khaldun crafted the most theoretically sustained reading of "History" as an autonomous philosophical investigation. Mahdi has extensively argued Ibn Khaldun's full awareness of a principal epistemic distinction between juridical sciences (scholasticism in general) and the philosophical quest, under which he squarely places his study of history. In Mahdi's own words:

> According to Ibn Khaldun, prophecy is a human phenomenon: The prophet is a human being, his traits are human traits, his knowledge is human knowledge, his powers are human powers, his acts are human acts, and his purpose is a human purpose. This does not mean that every human being is a prophet or can become a prophet through learning or practicing a certain art. Nor does it exclude what the Muslims called "divine selection." On the contrary, Ibn Khaldun believes that prophecy is, in a sense, the highest form of human existence. The prophet is an extremely rare individual who must possess special, and rarely attainable, natural powers from birth, and lead a correct life prior to, and during, his mission as a prophet. Consequently, to explain the phenomenon of prophecy, Ibn Khaldun enquires into the nature of man and attempts to show how a human being becomes a prophet.[60]

Based on this historical humanization of the sacrosanct in the Qur'anic imagination, Ibn Khaldun ushers in a full systematic treatment of an evident fact implicit in the earliest historiographical records, from the time long before Ibn Khaldun, that Ibn Ishaq wrote the Prophet's biography, to the time that al-Tabari wrote his magnum *Ta'rikh al-Rusul wa al-Muluk (History of Prophets and Kings)*. Having Ibn Khaldun's philosophical history in mind, and having had to resort to an oxymoronic expression, Mahdi's conclusion after a careful reading of Ibn Khaldun is the fact "that Islamic philosophy—quite independently of the decisive changes of perspective that took place in European thought in the sixteenth and seventeenth centuries—was capable of being much more secular, political, and realistic, than he [Muhsin Mahdi] had assumed."[61] "Islamic philosophy," to the degree that it can be "Islamic," can never be "secular"—nor indeed vice versa, for the whole binary is flawed. The fact that Ibn Khaldun's philosophy of history, as indeed the entire philosophical tradition from Aristotle to Averroes and beyond, is "secular," that is, executed on an epistemic space adjacent to the Biblical metanarrative in general and the sacred Qur'anic memory in particular, makes the very proposition of the Islamicity of that culture problematic. It is the Muslims *worldly* civilization that embraces Ibn Khaldun's philosophy of history and the Qur'anic metanarrative together without the slightest

DOI: 10.1057/9781137301291

contradiction. Ibn Khaldun's is not an "Islamic philosophy of history," if the adjectival "Islamic" is to a have a reference to the epistemic authority of the Qur'an as a commanding metanarrative. Beyhaqi as a literary humanist and Ibn Khaldun as a philosopher of history were among the key architects of an historical imagination constitutionally *worldly* in the widest and most common understanding of the term.

A geographical imagination

From history we can move to geography for an even fuller reading of that worldliness—this time literally. A highly cultivated "geographical imagination," evident in, indeed made possible through, a rich literature made the medieval inhabitants of lands to the south and east of the Mediterranean Sea—deep into Central Asia and all the way to India and China—highly conscious of cultures far beyond the absolutist claims of any particular faith. The gradual construction of this imagination was not only irreducible to any religion but in fact was quite corrosive to any absolutist claims of one particular faith. This expansive geographical imagination that included Muslim lands but was not limited to them is the locus classicus of Muslim consciousness and worldliness.

That geographical imagination was integral to an open-ended liberal disposition in higher learning. Ibn Wadih al-Ya'qubi (flourished around 864), the father of geographical literature in Arabic,[62] was not only a geographer and historian, but also an astronomer and a poet, that is, a model Adab humanist. Al-Ya'qubi wrote extensively on the geography of the Byzantine Empire, the African conquest of Muslims, and the Byzantine emperors, as well as the treatise "The History of Ancient People." Probably composed by 892, the surviving parts of *al-Buldan* show its author's global conception of an imaginative geography in which by the late ninth century Muslims thought themselves living.

It is quite evident that by the time Ibn Hawqal (flourished 977) wrote his *Sawrat al-Ard* there was already a significant literature on geography that fascinated him and deeply informed his work. As Ibn Hawqal puts it: "I wished to know [other] people's various customs, habits, [forms of] knowledge, sciences, and religions."[63] He wrote his book on geography in part because he was not satisfied with the existing literature. During the same era, by 982, the geographical literature was already so rich that the unknown author of *Hudud al-Alam min al-Mashriq ila al-Maghrib*

DOI: 10.1057/9781137301291

composed the book "The Frontiers of the World from the East to the West"—one of the earliest extant texts in Persian language following the Islamic conquest.[64] A global conception of the world is the context in which the author of *Hudud al-Alam* knew, for example, that the earth was round: "The earth is round, just like a ball, and the heavens surround it. It turns on two poles, one called the North Pole, the other the South Pole."[65]

The expansive geographical imagination of this early period continued into later ages. Early in the fourteenth century Abu al-Fida's *Taqwim al-Buldan* is a perfect example of the most detailed geographical knowledge on a global scale.[66] *Taqwim al-Buldan* provides extensive geographical information on every civilized corner of the world—from China to India, Transoxiana, Europe, and Armenia, to Persia, Arabia, Syria, Andalusia, and Africa. After that, the geographical part of *Nuzhat al-Qolub*, composed in 1340 by Hamdollah al-Mawstawfi, the author of the celebrated *Ta'rikh-e Gozideh*,[67] shows the geography of one particular land and culture, in this case Iran, is narrated with a framing attention to a global geography. There is, in effect, no consciousness of any Muslim land independent of that global geography.

This massive geographical literature was augmented by an equally important body of travel narratives. Toward the middle of the fourteenth century, Ibn Battuta (1304–1368) had written one of the most celebrated travelogues of the medieval period. Starting his journey from Morocco, he traveled to Egypt, Syria, Arabia, Persia, Asia Minor, the eastern part of Europe, Transoxiana, the Indian subcontinent, China, and back to some parts of Africa—carrying with him and recording a global conception of his worldly being.[68] From the heart of Africa to the frontiers of China became the subject of Ibn Battuta's insights, elements of a global conception of communities, societies, polities, cultures, and civilizations, constitutionally irreducible to any particular faith or doctrine. This body of literature represents a cosmovision of reality that is not subsumed by "Islam," but embraces it, and upon which perception Muslims have historically known themselves.

Heresiographical imagination

Linked to this geographical imagination is an equally extensive "heresiographical imagination" which has produced the most extensive literature on various religions, sects, cultures, and philosophies. To be sure, the

DOI: 10.1057/9781137301291

origin of this genre is rooted in sectarian movements within the Qur'anic imagination. But very soon attraction to and interest in religions and philosophies become realities sui generis.

Notable among the earliest heresiographical sources in which full attention is paid to the varieties of sectarian movements are *Firaq al-Shi'ah* of al-Nawbakhti (d. 912), *al-Maqalat wa al-Firaq* of Sa'd ibn Abdullah abi Khalaf al-Ash'ari (d. 913), *Maqalat al-Islamiyyn fi Ikhtilaf al-Musaliyyn* of Abu al-Hasan al-Ash'ari (d. 935), *al-Tanbih wa al-Radd ala Ahl Ahwa' wa al-Bida'* of Abd al-Rahman al-Multi (d. 987). Extended from the prover- bial Prophetic parable of "seventy-two" sects into which Muslims will be divided, these sources are often written from the polemical perspective of a staunch supporter of one ("orthodox") position. Although often meant to legitimize and authenticate the "orthodox" position of their authors, these heresiographical texts have had the unintended consequence of making their readers aware of the varieties of interpretations to which one particular revelatory language can be subjected. This effective historical hermeneutics led to polemical engagements with non-"orthodox" read- ing of the faith already predicated on the assumption of their multisig- nificatory nature. The more vigorously the advocates of one "orthodoxy" or another argued their case against all other "heterodoxies," the more self-evident became the multisignificatory reality of Qur'anic revelation. The dialogical nature of faith as an intersection between history and doctrine also became evident in this heresiographical literature. Almost all early sectarian movements emerged as doctrinal/political responses to a specific historical event, whether it was the question of succession to Prophet Muhammad's authority, the murder of the third Rightly-Guided caliph Uthman, acceptance of arbitration by Ali after his victory over Mu'awiyah, or any other seminal turning point in post-Muhammadan history. The results were the same—the inner, organic, expansion of Muslims' worldliness in correspondence with the material realities that had occasioned their sectarianism.

By the eleventh and twelfth centuries the study of religions, sects, cul- tures, and philosophies beyond the doctrinal acceptance and tolerance of "Islam" reached their highest zenith. When Abu Mansur al-Baghdadi (d. 1038) wrote his *al-Farq bayn al-Firaq* he was already aware of the influ- ence of Greek (Neo-Platonic), Iranian (Zoroastrian and Manichean), Christian (Gnostic and Ascetic), and Jewish influences on the formation of sectarian movements within the "Islamic" tradition proper.[69] Equally evident in al-Baghdadi's account is an acute awareness of material

DOI: 10.1057/9781137301291

history in the formation of sectarian movements. Although al-Baghdadi remained a staunch Sunni and radically polemical in presenting his opponents' ideas and doctrines, a panoramic conception of the historical unfolding of the Qur'anic memory and of the Muhammadan legacy is unmistakable in his text. Clustered around the generic categories of Shi'ites, Murji'ites, Mu'tazilites, and a host of other groups, is a galaxy of doctrinal and dogmatic interpretations of the Muhammadan prophetic mission, all in direct negotiation with specific historical events. Many of these sectarian movements are identified with specific individuals— Kamiliyyah with Abi Kamil, Nawusiyyah with Nawus, Shumaytiyyah with Yahya' ibn Shumayt, all of them among the Shi'ites. Quite inadvertently, al-Baghdadi demonstrates the phenomenal subjectivity of these sectarian movements, in which latent potentialities of the Qur'anic and Muhammadan memories, specific historical forces, and individual encounters with matters of faith and piety have led to a multiplicity of voices and visages of the sacred, all, without any exception, having claim to Absolute Truth.

Produced in the same century, but far superior in its critical apparatus, was the monumental *al-Fasl fi al-Milal wa al-Ahwa' wa al-Nihal*, by Spain's great scholar Ibn Hazm al-Andalusi (d. 1063). Of either Persian or Spanish descent, Ibn Hazm represented the crowning achievement of Arabic culture and civilization in Spain; he was prodigiously learned and an Adab humanist par excellence. But his *al-Fasl fi al-Milal wa al-'Ahwa wa al-Nihal* is by far his greatest work, "which entitles him to the honor of being the first scholar in the field of comparative religion."[70] Hitti in fact suggests that not until the rise of textual criticism in the sixteenth century do we see any scholar raising the sorts of critical questions raised by Ibn Hazm on biblical narratives. Ibn Hazm paid no attention to the customary division of sects into "seventy-three" and sought to distinguish among them on principal matters of doctrine and conviction. He was instrumental in transforming the knowledge of Muslim sects into a doctrinal expansion of their emotive universe.

Halfway through the twelfth century, the appearance of *al-Milal wa al-Nihal* of al-Shahrastani (d. 1153) points to even more elaborate, impartial, and critical studies in comparative religions and philosophies.[71] The production of *al-Milal wa al-Nihal* in the twelfth century already points to the active fragmentation of "Islamic societies" into sectarian divisions radically hostile to each other. The Fatimids in Egypt and the Zaydis in Tabarestan, not to mention the Isma'ilis, who were just about everywhere

DOI: 10.1057/9781137301291

and who challenged not only the central authority of the caliphate and their Saljuq warlords, but on a more serious level questioned the nomo-centric definition of the faith by the Sunni clerical establishment. The fact that a great theologian like Abu Hamid al-Ghazali felt obligated to denounce the Isma'ilis in a number of his treatises is a solid indication that this particular reading of the Qur'anic narratives had shaken the Sunni establishment to its roots. In the meantime, the presence of Jewish, Christian, Hindu, Buddhist, Zoroastrian, and Manichaean communities in the immediate neighborhood of Muslims further fragmented the active consciousness of alternative claims to absolutist "Truth."

Al-Shahrastani's *al-Milal wa al-Nihal* is by far the most daring attempt to put together an encyclopedic compendium of world religions and philosophies. In his introductory remarks, al-Shahrastani points out that some of his contemporaries prefer to divide the people of the world according to the clime in which they live and habits and customs that they form. Thus they will stipulate certain characteristics for the inhabitants of every clime according to which they define and understand them. Others divide the world and its inhabitants into the four geographical directions of East, West, North, and South, and then describe the inhabitants of these regions in terms of their differing natures and ways of life. Still others have divided people into four "nations" (*ummah*): the Arabs, the Persians, the Romans, and the Indians. The Indians and the Arabs are close to each other in their way of thinking, as are the Persians and the Romans. Arabs and Indians tend to describe the essence and attributes of things and their practical applications, while Persians and Romans are more inclined to understand the nature of things and to describe the philosophical what-ness and howness of them. Finally, there are also those who divide the people of the earth according to their religion and faith. It is in this latter respect that al-Shahrastani wishes to divide the people of the world.

The defining factor for al-Shahrastani in his division of world religions and philosophies reveals the remarkable liberality of his imagination. He divided all religions and philosophies not according to their puta-tive proximity to "Truth," but based on whether or not they believed in a revealed text. In matters of ideas and convictions, then, people are divided into three groups: those who believe in a revealed text, those who believe in a pseudo-text, and those who do not believe in any text. Jews, Christians, and Muslims share a belief in a revealed text. Zoroastrians, Manichaeans, and Mazdakites believe in a pseudo-text. Greek and Muslim philosophers do not believe in a revealed text and follow their

DOI: 10.1057/9781137301291

own judgment in matters of ideas and dogmas. It is rather remarkable that al-Shahrastani categorizes both Greek and Muslim philosophers as those who do not believe in a revealed text.[72] Plato and Aristotle, as a result, are in the same category as Alfarabi and Avicenna. In the same category are also considered the Indian philosophers.

Al-Shahrastani's *al-Milal wa al-Nihal* was extremely influential in medieval and even modern history. After its initial composition in Arabic in 1127, it was translated into Persian by Afdal al-Din Sadr Turkah al-Isfahani (d. 1446) in 1439. In 1611–1612 Mustafa ibn Khaleqdad Hashemi thumm al-Abbasi, commissioned by the Mughal emperor Jahangir, re-narrated al-Isfahani's translation. A Turkish translation appeared in 1659 by Nuh ibn Mustafa.[73] All these renditions are indices that the text deeply complicated the worldly disposition of their collective Muslim faith.

The composition of a text like *Haftad-o Seh Mellat* by an unknown author sometime in the fourteenth century[74] indicates the interests of Sufi heresiographers in co-opting the legitimizing narrative. While the same putative Prophetic Hadith of "seventy-three" sects continues to function as the basis of this treatise, the felicity of the post-thirteenth-century Persian prose is used here effectively to poeticize sectarian divisions. Although a Sunni Muslim himself, the author demonstrates a remarkable liberality in his treatment of other sects, while demonstrating a noticeable self-constraint in praising his own faith.[75]

The rich heresiographical literature in Arabic, Persian, and other neighboring languages points to a universal awareness of religions and philosophies beyond any essentialist assumption of or about "Islam." A comparative awareness of world religions, a simultaneous attention to non-religious philosophical schools, a universal conception of nations and their ideas, are among the salient features of this literature and they all point to a phenomenally potent force shattering the categorical claim of "Islam" on any community thus identified. Muslims were Muslims not merely by virtue of any scholastic conviction in one sect or another, but, far from it, by virtue of a universal awareness of the communal contingency of truth.

Agnostic imagination

A perfectly "agnostic imagination," immediately identified with the two great poets al-Ma'arri and Omar Khayyam, has been a principal ingredient of that effervescent culture we are used to calling "Islamic." Abu al-Ala al-Ma'arri (973–1058) is by far the most eloquent voice in medieval Arabic agnostic imagination. In his prose and poetry, life and thought, al-Ma'arri's defied Qur'anic dogmas and challenged the doctrinal foundations of Muslim beliefs. With a moral courage unrivaled in his environment, al-Ma'arri defied the "Islamic orthodoxy" and spoke the not-so-silent thoughts of generations of literary humanists. He had a vision of this world and he was eloquent in expressing it. His remarkable courage in speaking about his doubts, and thus defining the sentiment of generations of readers who choose to remember and celebrate him, prompted one observer to consider him "one of the greatest moralists of all time whose profound genius anticipated much that is commonly attributed to the so-called modern spirit of enlightenment."[76] Targeting the most sacrosanct in "Islamic Orthodoxy," al-Ma'arri would sing:

We laugh, but inept is our laughter;

> We should weep and weep sore,
> Who are shattered like glass, and thereafter
> Re-mould no more.[77]

His kindred spirit in Persian poetry, Omar Khayyam (1048–1131), would echo precisely the same sentiment, defying precisely the same doctrines of sacred certitude:

> Oh, come with old Khayyam, and leave the Wise
> To talk; one thing is certain, that Life flies;
> One thing is certain, and the Rest is Lies;
> The Flower that once has blown for ever dies.[78]

Al-Ma'arri would equate all expressions of religious fanaticism and opt for an ironic twist to the very cast of reality:

> Hanifs are stumbling, Christians all astray,
> Jews wildered, Magians far on error's way.
> We mortals are composed of two great schools—
> Enlightened knaves or else religious fools.[79]

Omar Khayyam's reading follows the same sentiments into the Persian domain:

> Why, all the Saints and Sages who discuss'd
> Of the Two Worlds so learnedly, are thrust
> Like foolish Prophets forth; their Words to Scorn
> Are scattere'd, and their Mouths are stop with Dust.[80]

DOI: 10.1057/9781137301291

Al-Ma'arri's denunciation of religious bigotry could be dark:

> Falsehood hath so corrupted all the world
> That wrangling sects each other's gospel chide;
> But were not hate Man's natural element,
> Churches and mosques had risen side by side.[81]

While Omar Khayyam's quite jubilant:

> The Grape that can with Logic absolute
> The Two-and-Seventy jarring Sects confute:
> The subtle Alchemist that in a Trice
> Life's leaden Metal into Gold transmute.[82]

But constant in them both is a festive celebration of life before and beyond its dogmatic codification and religious sectarianism. In the agnostic imagination that al-Ma'arri and Omar Khayyam represent and celebrate we witness a culture of life and liberty, a poetics of emancipation, radically at odds with every grain of the juridical regimentation of a "religious life." Omar Khayyam and al-Ma'arri were also Muslims, and their agnostic imagination integral to Muslim worldliness.

Scientific imagination

How can we account for the astonishing scientific achievements of the Muslim world? A varied and pervasive "scientific imagination" characterizes the intellectual culture of this world. This scientific imagination is by no stretch of imagination reducible to Islamic scholasticism. It is the material foundation of a vast empire, particularly during the Abbasids, that can account for the range of scientific undertakings in these societies. To be sure, certain limited objectives of scientific inquiry were used for a religious purpose. For example, the science of astronomy had certain limited uses in the mosque in relation to the Muslim calendar, setting the juridically stipulated times of prayers, and so on. But an astrophysicist like Khwajah Nasir al-Din al-Tusi (1201–1274) could equally serve the mundane needs of his Isma'ili or Mongol princes and warlords. The scientific activities these scientists were engaged in were not limited to their practical implications for the mosque or the court. In fact, we know that such scientists as al-Tusi used their influence with their patron princes in order to extend their scientific inquiry far beyond

DOI: 10.1057/9781137301291

religious or political mandates. The scientific imagination actively operative in such cases became a reality sui generis, yet with far reaching implications for the character and culture of the Muslim worldliness.

Without any exception, all medieval historians and practitioners of science, from al-Khwarazmi in the ninth century to Ibn Khaldun in the fourteenth, have distinguished between "religious" and "non-religious" sciences (*Ulum*). In his brief encyclopedia of sciences produced in the ninth century, al-Khwarazmi, for example, categorically distinguished between what he then called "the sciences of the Islamic religious law and the Arabic sciences connected with it, and...the sciences originating from foreigners such as the Greek[s] and other nations."[83] While al-Khwarazmi considered such subjects as jurisprudence and speculative theology to be the proper domains of "Islamic sciences," he thought that philosophy, logic, medicine, arithmetic, geometry, astronomy-astrology, music, mechanics, and alchemy had nothing to do with Islam, because they had originated in other domains. Their current practitioners were of course Muslim (just as Galileo was Christian and Einstein Jewish). But the sciences themselves, al-Khwarazmi thought, originated in non-Islamic domains and thus continued in a manner unrelated to Islamic scholasticism. A Muslim scientist or philosopher may very well have prayed five times a day, fasted during the month of Ramadan, paid his religious dues, and even performed his Hajj pilgrimage. Others, Avicenna, the Muslim scientist and philosopher *par excellence*, a prime example of them, may have publicly recorded their taste for forbidden wine and illicit sex.[84] But neither that religious piety nor its opposite had anything to do with their scientific and philosophical practices as an astrophysicist or an Aristotelian, for example. The normative and epistemic foregrounding of these scientists were materially grounded and worldly in disposition. These were Muslim scientists, but what they produced was not "Islamic science"—to come to terms with that fact is to come to terms with the worldly consciousness of how Muslims have been in the world.

A century after al-Khwarazmi, when al-Farabi (circa 872–950) wrote his *Ihsa' al-Ulum*, he altogether left out any reference to "religious sciences" and divided all sciences as such into five categories: linguistics, logic, mathematics (which included arithmetic, geometry, optics, mathematical astronomy, music, technology, and mechanics), the natural sciences, and politics. It is into the category of politics, that al-Farabi places jurisprudence and speculative theology.[85] This is an extraordinarily significant division, because the most sacrosanct "Islamic sciences," that is, Islamic

DOI: 10.1057/9781137301291

law and Islamic theology, are in fact sub-categorized under an Aristotelian division. How, then, anyone can call the sciences thus categorized "Islamic" in any meaningful way is beyond comprehension. Al-Farabi was a Muslim, but what he did was not "Islamic philosophy." He, like all Muslim thinkers, was located squarely within his worldly disposition, and everything he thought and did, including his faith, was embedded in that worldliness.

To be sure, "Islamic sciences" do return to medieval classification of sciences as a distinct category later in the tenth century. In their *Rasa'il*, the Ikhwan al-Safa' (961–986) divided everything that there was to know into three genera of sciences: "the propaedeutic sciences, the conventional sciences of the religious law and the real philosophical sciences."[86] The Brethren of Purity further elaborate that "the propaedeutic sciences consist of those disciplines which were mainly created in order to assure a livelihood and to promote worldly prosperity," such as "writing and reading" or "magic, talisman, alchemy, mechanics and the like." "The sciences of the religious law," on the other hand are those "that were created for the healing of souls and for the quest for future life," such as "the science of the Revelation" or "jurisprudence." "The philosophical sciences," however, "consist of four kinds: (a) the propaedeutic-mathematical, (b) the logical, (c) the natural and (d) the metaphysical sciences."[87] What is remarkable about this particular division of sciences is that the exclusive subject of "religious sciences" is bracketed between "the philosophical sciences" and "the propaedeutic sciences," that is, sciences that have to do with the material life. From "writing and reading" to "lexicography and grammar"; "arithmetic as required for bookkeeping and commerce"; "poetry and prosody"; "augury, omens and the like"; "magic, talismans, alchemy, mechanics and the like"; "trades and crafts"; "retail and wholesale trade, agriculture and animal husbandry"; and finally. "biography and history," a series of professional sciences were enumerated by the Brethren of Purity that had nothing to do with the dogmatic principals and the revelatory language of their Holy Text. Thus by the tenth century professional and philosophical sciences represented the range of economic and intellectual engagements and interests among Muslims beyond their religiously required knowledge of jurisprudence or theology. All of these indicate that the material expansion of Muslim empires had created a worldly disposition into which Muslims incorporated their knowledge of their faith, rather than the other way around.

A remarkable evidence for the worldly disposition of non-religious sciences is to be found in the eleventh-century philosopher Ibn Hazm's

DOI: 10.1057/9781137301291

(994–1064) classification of sciences. In his *Maratib al-Ulum*, Ibn Hazm maintained that:

> At all times and in all nations everywhere the sciences have been divided into seven parts. The first three are (1) the science of the religious law as possessed by every nation, since every nation has some belief, which can be positive or negative, (2) the history of the nation concerned and (3) the science of the language it speaks. The various nations all differ from one another in respect of these three sciences. The remaining four sciences, however, are the same everywhere, namely (4) astronomy, (5) arithmetic, (6) medicine, that is, concern with the human body, and (7) philosophy.[88]

What is significant in Ibn Hazm's formulation is the specific reference to the fact that non-religious sciences are irreducible to the faith, language, or history of a people. In other words, in Ibn Hazm's estimation, science is science whether it is practiced by Asians, Africans, or Europeans, by Jews, Christians, or Muslims, in Hebrew, Latin, or Arabic. Even more specifically, it is in his or her faith, language, or historical memory that a Muslim is a Muslim (here we need to bracket for the moment the fact that even in this respect there are subdivisions because a Muslim Indian or Iranian or Turk shares Islam with his or her Arab fellow-Muslims but not in language or historical memory). In matters of scientific inquiry then, according to Ibn Hazm's classification, neither science is reducible to faith, language or history, nor can there be a "Jewish philosophy," a "Christian philosophy" or an "Islamic philosophy." Water boils and freezes at a certain degree, the human body responds with fever to a virus, and the earth rotates around the sun with certain regularity, whether the observer speaks Hebrew and has a yarmulke on his head, Arabic and a turban, or Latin and a cross hanging around his neck. It is the worldly disposition of scientists and philosophers that determines the normative but changing epistemes of their knowledge production, not in which direction they may or may not pray.

Ibn Hazm was perfectly aware of the way aspects of worldly sciences could be used either in support of the veracity of religion or against it. When discussing "rhetoric," for example, he noted:

> When applied in the service of God and for clarifying the realities as well as for the instruction of the ignorant, rhetoric is a virtue. But when applied for opposite purposes, it is a useless business, an expenditure of effort and a waste of life on something harmful—may God protect us from such a calamity.[89]

DOI: 10.1057/9781137301291

Obviously, for "rhetoric" to have the ability to either serve or subvert public piety, it must have an autonomous entity independent of "Islam"—and there cannot be anything like "Islamic logic" or "Islamic rhetoric."

Once again, in the eleventh century, in the *Kitab al-Najah* of Avicenna (circa 980–1037), we note a classification of sciences that has no reference to religious knowledge. "The sciences," according to Avicenna:

> are either different from one another or related to one another. The sciences that are different from one another are those whose objects have nothing to do with one another in respect of either their essence or their genus, for example arithmetic and natural science. The sciences related to one another are either of equal rank, or some are contained in others, or some are subordinate to others. Sciences of equal ranks are, for instance, geometry and arithmetic which have objects of related genus, since both spatial extension and numbers are a kind of quantity; or natural science and astronomy, since they have one and the same objects, namely, the world, but regard it from different points of view, since astronomy regards it from the point of view of its movement and rest, combination and separation, etc., which has generally somehow to do with quality, whereas natural science regards it [the world] from the point of view of the quantification of its essence and accidents. Hence, natural science and astronomy have most problems in common, but the reasoning of astronomy produces causal relationships, while that of natural science establishes the facts of existence. Furthermore, astronomical reasoning starts from an active cause, while that of natural science starts from a formal cause.[90]

Here, we observe a complete takeover of the rational sub-division of sciences by principles and variables exclusively related to their subject matter. In this classification, Avicenna's concern is entirely limited to the way worldly sciences relate to each other, with questions such as why "music" is a subdivision of "arithmetic" and not of "natural science." What this indicates is that certainly by Avicenna's time, the scientific imagination had already assumed a reality entirely sui generis, to the degree that it was no longer necessary to define worldly sciences in terms of their distinction from religious sciences.

The distinction between "religious sciences" and "philosophical science," though, was ultimately preserved throughout the medieval world and ultimately received its stamp of approval by Ibn Khaldun in the fourteenth century.[91] But Ibn Khaldun's wording in distinguishing between the two is marvelously precise:

> It should be known that the sciences with which people concern themselves in cities and which they acquire and pass on through instruction, are of two

DOI: 10.1057/9781137301291

kinds: one that is natural to man and to which he is guided by his own ability to think, and a traditional kind that he learns from those who invented it. The first kind comprises the philosophical sciences....The second kind comprises the traditional, conventional sciences.[92]

Bibliographical imagination

In the year 987, a Baghdadi bookseller, Ibn Nadim (d. 995), put together a remarkably annotated bibliography that he simply called *al-Fihrist* ("the List"). It is because of this extraordinary piece of evidence that today we can talk about a "bibliographical imagination" that was particularly conducive to an open-minded worldly conception of the Muslims universe. In the introduction to his *al-Fihrist*, Ibn Nadim very simply said that his principal objective in bringing this book together was to provide a list of "all the books of all the nations, whether Arab or non-Arab, composed in various scientific disciplines, available in the language and script of Arabic."[93] Ibn Nadim's obvious encyclopedic command over his material is most immediately evident in the way he classifies his bibliography. He begins his first chapter with a thorough review of world languages and scripts and orthographies. It is under this linguistic division that Ibn Nadim addresses the world religions and their sacred texts, paying particular attention to the Qur'an and Qur'anic studies. The second chapter is on grammar, both syntax and morphology. As it is immediately evident from the first two chapters of *al-Fihrist*, Ibn Nadim's classification is not in any way based on either the Qur'anic revelation, nor is it exclusive to the Muslim community. On the contrary, he opts to narrate his bibliography entirely on the basis of a neutral linguistic principle. To be sure, Ibn Nadim is a Muslim, as it is perfectly clear in his praise of and preference for the Qur'an. But his faith notwithstanding, when it comes to his professional competence as a librarian, bookseller, and now, bibliographer an entirely worldly imagination takes over, and he proceeds from a premise that has nothing to do with his religion—thus placing that religion within Ibn Nadim's cosmopolitan conception of himself.

Ibn Nadim's third chapter is on history and culture, and includes biographies of famous people, from powerful kings to famous jesters, who are mentioned in regard to books they have written or have had written about them. From language, grammar, and history, Ibn Nadim's attention then turns to poetry and poets. Here too, Ibn Nadim's attention is

DOI: 10.1057/9781137301291

drawn first to pre-Islamic poets and then to poets of the Islamic period. It is only after his chapter on the poets and poetry that Ibn Nadim turns to theology and theologians. It is as if in his mind the poets have the same relation to language as theologians have to sacred texts, and as language comes before sacred texts, so does poetry come before theology. From theology, Ibn Nadim moves naturally to law, jurisprudence, and Prophetic traditions, before he turns his attention to philosophy and what he calls "ancient sciences." Three chapters later, Ibn Nadim's treatment of philosophy is quite noteworthy. His categories of philosophy are, in order of his preference, "superstition and magic," "religious beliefs," and "alchemy." Under "superstition and magic," Ibn Nadim includes storytellers, superstition narrators, painters, magicians, sorcerers, and so on. Under "religious beliefs" he places such topics as the religion of the Manicheans and the Mazdakites, as well as the religions of India and China. Under "alchemy," Ibn Nadim gives a thorough bibliographical account of those alchemists who have pursued the science of making gold and silver through the chemical reactions of metals against each other, rather than mining. These last three categories are for Ibn Nadim "suspicious" sciences, the veracity of which he does not vouchsafe.

When we consider the ten chapters into which Ibn Nadim divides his bibliography in the tenth century, an encyclopedic awareness of the modes of knowledge production becomes evident that is paramount in its author's bibliographical imagination. Dominant in that imagination are the epistemic premises from which varieties of knowledge emerge. What we may today call "religious science" is one among a number of other modes of knowledge production, with no particular advantage or disadvantage. To be sure, as a Muslim, Ibn Nadim privileges the position of the Qur'anic revelation over all other religious traditions. But "religion" as such constitutes one of a number of other epistemic premises upon which a mode of knowledge is predicated. Subtextually, there is a hierarchy in Ibn Nadim's bibliographical imagination. He predicates every mode of knowledge on language. Without language, there is no other mode of knowledge, including the religious. Of language, Ibn Nadim has a thoroughly worldly, and even orthographic, conception, beginning his description of language from the outer appearance of scripts. While language is at the top of Ibn Nadim's hierarchy, such "suspicious sciences" as superstition, magic, sorcery, and alchemy are on the bottom. It is as if he begins with the most evident and concludes with the most suspicious, and in between are the varieties of ways in which humans have produced knowledge.

DOI: 10.1057/9781137301291

A renewed worldliness

Being a Muslim in a post-Western world necessitates a critical thinking that will gloss over the colonial and post-colonial experiences, whereby Muslims were turned into the ideological instruments of political resistance in European imperialism. A critical rethinking of Islamic cosmopolitanism does not require a "reformation" modeled on that of European Christianity, but a restoration of that spirit of worldliness in which being a Muslim meant embracing, rather than rejecting, the world. Muslims lived that worldliness over many centuries and produced a massive global civilization as its enduring trace. The possibilities of inhabiting the renewed worldliness of Muslims' lived experiences is contingent on a full-bodied recognition of the multiple varieties of creative and critical imaginations that collectively inform the medieval Muslim mind and the world Muslims had envisioned around themselves. We need to remember the past well in order to be able to live in a full-bodied future. Instead of a false and flawed "dialogue" with a "West" that no longer exists, we need to have a dialogue with our own pre-Western past that we have actively forgotten.

Notes

1   F. E. Peters, *Aristotle and the Arabs: The Aristotelian Tradition in Islam* (New York: New York University Press, 1968): xvii–xviii.
2   See George Makdisi, *The Rise of Humanism in Classical Islam and the Christian West: With Special Reference to Scholasticism* (Edinburgh: Edinburgh University Press, 1990).
3   *Encyclopedia of Islam*, c.v. "ADAB".
4   Ibid.
5   Ibid.
6   Makdisi 1990: 89.
7   Ibid: 90.
8   Quoted in Makdisi 1990: 90.
9   Ibid: 88.
10 Ibn Nadim, *Kitab al-Fihrist*. Edited and translated by M. Reza Tajaddod (Tehran: Bank Bazargani Iran, 1967): 3–6.
11 Al-Farabi, *Ihsa' al-'Ulum*. Edited and translated by Hossein Khadiv Jam (Tehran: Sherkat Entesharat Elmi va Farhangi, 1969): 106–119.
12 Muhammad ibn Ali al-Sakaki, *Miftah al-'Ulum* (Beirut: Dar al-Kutub, 1983).

DOI: 10.1057/9781137301291

13   Makdisi 1990: xix.
14   Ibid: xix.
15   Ibid: xx.
16   Ibid: xx.
17   Ibid: 93.
18   Ibid: 94–95.
19   Quoted in Makdisi 1990: 92.
20   Ibid: 92.
21   Ibid: 92.
22   Ibid: 113.
23   Ibid: 113.
24   Ibid: 94.
25   Ibid: 114.
26   EI, c.v., "ADAB".
27   Makdisi 1990: 90.
28   R. A. Nicholson, *A Literary History of the Arabs* (London: Curzon Press, 1907): 344.
29   Makdisi 1990: 112.
30   EI, c. v. "ADAB."
31   H. A. R. Gibb, *Studies on the Civilization of Islam* (Boston: Beacon Press, 1962): 62.
32   For more on the early formation of this charismatic force see Hamid Dabashi, *Authority in Islam: From the Rise of Muhammad to the Establishment of the Umayyads* (New Brunswick, NJ: Transactions, 1989).
33   See Thorstein Veblen, *The Theory of the Leisure Class* (London: Penguin Classics, 1994).
34   Gibb 1962: 66.
35   Nicholson 1907: 292.
36   Nicholson 1907: 296–298.
37   Von Kremer as quoted in Nicholson 1907: 316.
38   Quoted in Nicholson 1907: 318.
39   Naser Khosrow, *Safarnameh* (Tehran: Jibi Publications, 1971): 14–15.
40   See Badi' al-Zaman Foruzanfar, *Sokhan va Sokhanvaran* (Tehran: Khwarazmi, 1929–1933): 44–51.
41   George Marçais as quoted in Oleg Grabar, *The Formation of Islamic Art* (New Haven, CT: Yale University Press, 1973): 1.
42   Grabar 1973: 1.
43   Grabar 1973: 1–2.
44   Grabar 1973: 2.
45   Ibid.
46   See N. J. Dawood, *Tales from the Arabian Nights* (New York: Doubleday, 1954): 7.

DOI: 10.1057/9781137301291

47 Dawood 1954: 8.
48 Dawood 1954: 8.
49 See Mia I. Gerhardt, *The Art of Story-telling: A Literary Study of the Thousand and One Nights* (Leiden: E. J. Brill, 1963): 3–4.
50 Gerhardt 1963: 4.
51 See Faramarz ibn Khodad ibn Abdollah al-Kateb al-Arjani, *Samak Ayyar*, 5 vols. Edited and annotated with an introduction by Parviz Natel Khanlari (Tehran: Agah, 1983), I: 6.
52 Khanlari 1983, VI: 5.
53 Ibid, V: 92.
54 Marilyn R. Waldman, *Toward a Theory of Historical Narrative: A Case Study in Perso-Islamicate Historiography* (Columbus: Ohio State University, 1980): 131.
55 In Mary Louise Pratt, *Toward a Speech Act Theory of Literary Discourse* (Bloomington, IN: Indiana University Press, 1977): 136.
56 Waldman 1980: 133.
57 Ibid: 132.
58 Ibid.
59 Muhsin Mahdi, *Ibn Khaldun's Philosophy of History: A Study in the Philosophic Foundation of the Science of Culture* (Chicago: University of Chicago Press, 1957).
60 Mahdi 1957: 85.
61 Ibid: 6.
62 See Muhammad Ibrahim Ayati's *Introduction to Ahmad ibn al-Ya'qubi, al-Buldan* (Tehran: Bongah Tarjomeh va Nashr-e Ketab, 1963): 9–17.
63 Ibn Hawqal, *Surat al-Ard*. Edited and translated into Persian, with an introduction and commentary by Jafar Sha'ar (Tehran: Entesharat-e Bonyad-e Farhang, 1966): T.
64 Anonymous, *Hudud al-Alam min al-Mashriq ila al-Maghrib*. Edited by Manuchehr Sotudeh (Tehran: Tahuri Publishers, 1983).
65 Anonymous 1983: 8.
66 Abu al-Fida', *Taqwim al-Buldan*. Edited and translated into Persian, with an introduction and commentary by Abd al-Mohammad Ayati (Tehran: Entesharat-e Bonyad-e Farhang, 1970).
67 See Hamdollah Mawstawfi, *Nuzhat al-Qolub*. Edited by Guy le Strange (Tehran: Donya-ye Ketab, 1915).
68 Ibn Battuta, *The Adventures of Ibn Battuta: A Muslim Traveler of the Fourteenth Century* (Berkeley: University of California Press, 2004)
69 See Abu Mansur Abd al-Qadir al-Baghdadi, *Al-Farq bayn al-Firaq*. Edited and translated by Mohammad Javad Mashkur (Tehran: Ishraqi Publications, 1954).
70 Philip Hitti, *History of the Arabs* (New York: Palgrave Macmillan, 1970/2002): 558.

DOI: 10.1057/9781137301291

71   See Abu al-Fath Muhammad ibn Abd al-Karim al-Shahrastani, *al-Milal wa al-Nihal*. Edited and annotated by Seyyed Mohammad Reza Jalali Na'ini (Tehran: Offset Publications, 1979).

72   Al-Shahrastani 1979: 23–25.

73   Al-Shahrastani 1979: 77–78.

74   See Muhammad Javad Mashkur's introduction to Anonymous, *Haftad-o Seh Mellat* (Tehran: Ata'i Publications, 1962): 4.

75   Anonymous 1962: 76.

76   R. A. Nicholson, *A Literary History of the Arabs* (Cambridge: Cambridge University Press, 1907/1930): 316.

77   Quoted in Nicholson 1907: 316.

78   Omar Khayyam, *Ruba'iyat of Omar Khayyam*. Translated by Edward Fitzgerald (London: Penguin, 1989): 50.

79   Quoted in Nicholson 1907: 318.

80   Omar Khayyam 1989: 50.

81   Quoted in Nicholson 1907: 321.

82   Omar Khayyam 1989: 54.

83   Al-Khwarazmi as translated in Franz Rosenthal, *The Classical Heritage in Islam* (London: Routledge, 1975/1994): 54.

84   W. E. Gohlman, *The Life of Ibn Sina* (Albany: State University of New York Press, 1974): 29–31 and 81–83.

85   Rosenthal 1974: 54–55.

86   Rosenthal 1974: 56.

87   Rosenthal 1974: 56.

88   Rosenthal 1975: 60.

89   Rosenthal 1975: 60.

90   Rosenthal 1975: 61.

91   Ibn Khaldun, *The Muqaddimah*. Translated by Franz Rosenthal, 3 vols. (Princeton: Princeton University Press, 1958): II: 436–439.

92   Ibid: 436, emphasis added.

93   Ibn Nadim, *al-Fihrist*. Edited by Reza Tajaddod (Tehran: Amir Kabir, 1967): 3.

DOI: 10.1057/9781137301291

4
Being a Muslim

Abstract: *In Chapter 4, I argue that being a Muslim in the emerging worlds is both an ontological question and a proposition predicated on a radical re-thinking of the epistemic terms with which new regimes of knowledge might take shape. The formalism of the critical and creative faculties necessary to cultivate a language of existential self-awareness is contingent on the formal disposition of the language we will have to cultivate in conversation with the vital parameters of our renewed pact with post-Western history.*

Dabashi, Hamid. *Being a Muslim in the World.* New York: Palgrave Macmillan, 2013. DOI: 10.1057/9781137301291.

To be a Muslim in this world today, in this world and for any meaning-ful posterity, means being able to stand up and say, "I am a Muslim" and after that, to breathe comfortably, without looking over your shoul-der or waiting for the other shoe to drop. I live in a city in which to be a "Jewish intellectual" is proverbial to its history, yet a Muslim can-not be anything but a terrorist. The idea of a Muslim scholar, Muslim intellectual, Muslim feminist, Muslim Marxist, Muslim psychoanalyst, Muslim poststructuralist, Muslim postmodernist, or any other normal and varied moral and intellectual disposition that is connected to a person who is a Muslim has now been made entirely alien to this world we call home. To be a Muslim in this world begins by reclaiming those identities. It is in this city of New York—where the criminal atrocities of 9/11 happened—that one must stand up and say, "I am a Muslim." It is in London, where a band of Muslims has formed a "Council of ex-Muslims" that one must stand up and say, "I am a Muslim." It is in North America and Western Europe where one must get up and say "I am a Muslim." It is in Tehran, where another band of militant tyrants have laid exclusive claims on how to be a Muslim, and where they, as Muslims, have perpetrated criminal mass executions of political prison-ers and conducted repeated university purges, cultural revolutions, and systematic abuses of their own citizens, that one must, a fortiori, stand up and say, "I am a Muslim."

To be a Muslim is to own up to criminal atrocities that Muslims have done—and to stand up to those who are invested in blowing those atroci-ties out of proportion to justify even greater atrocities done to Muslims.

It is in Madrid, where another band of criminal Muslims have wreaked havoc on innocent people, and also in Mumbai, where yet another gang of Muslim terrorists went on a rampage and murdered countless innocent people, one must also stand up and say, "I am a Muslim." To be a Muslim in this world begins by categorically denouncing the nonsensical gibber-ish of Mahmoud Ahmadinejad denying the Holocaust—for no degree of commitment to and solidarity with the Palestinian cause can ever mean dismissing, denigrating, or disregarding the sufferings of millions of human beings—and this is precisely the way you will find the moral authority to denounce the pronouncements of Israeli prime minister Golda Meir, who, too, spoke gibberish when she said that "Palestinians do not exist." Millions of Jews perished during the European Holocaust, and millions of Palestinians were dispossessed and their land and had their liberty stolen from them by the Zionists. Having these two

DOI: 10.1057/9781137301291

simultaneous facts in mind is how we can begin to think how to be a Muslim in this world.

To be a Muslim in this world, you must be present in your words, invested in your ideas, committed to your location-in-the-world. You cannot talk about Muslims as "they" just because you are a Muslim who has Marxist leaning in her thinking, or is a feminist, gay, lesbian, or even if you have lost your way and the patience to find where in the world or in the heavens the Almighty God might be and call yourself an "atheist." If you are an atheist Muslim, well *Ahlen waSahlan*, welcome to the club! You might be an atheist Muslim, but you are a Muslim. Atheists, God bless them, can scarcely stop talking about God. And believing Muslims at least occasionally take a break: they regulate their time speaking about and to God to specified rituals called *salat* or *namaz* and such, and before and after that they think about other things. Atheists are more theists than they think. This is not to compromise their metaphysics of the unknown—just to mark it.

To accommodate a renewed understanding of the varieties of Muslims in the world, in the previous chapter I presented a panoramic view of Muslim societies through their intellectual productions by way of retrieving—narratively—the multifaceted cosmopolitan imagination in which Muslims were or became Muslims. Muslims were Muslims, I have argued, not merely by virtue of any scholastic conviction in one sect or another, the doctrinal rituals of which they followed in their daily lives, but—far from it—by virtue of a universal awareness (however subconscious) of the communal contingency of truth. We as Muslims must retrieve and celebrate that contingency in a renewed pact with our contemporary history.

"The most elementary forms of behavior motivated by religious or magical factors," Max Weber proposed, "are oriented to *this* world."[1] This world is the field upon which we cultivate, a Prophetic tradition has it, what we will crop in the world to come (*al-Dunyaka'l-Mazra'at al-Akhira'*). There is a definitive worldliness about Islam—has always been. Weber further noted: "Religious or magical behavior or thinking must not be set apart from the range of everyday purposive conduct, particularly since even the end of the religious and magical actions are predominantly economic."[2] This materiality is the frame of reference for all viable alterities that any intuition of transcendence might entail. Islam in particular, Weber noted: "'accommodated' itself to the world in a very unique sense."[3] Islam became a worldly religion from the moment of its

DOI: 10.1057/9781137301291

inception in Arabia and throughout its imperial expansion from the east to west of its birthplace. There is no other way to be a Muslim except to be a Muslim in the world.

That world, and thus any manner of accommodating it, is always contingent, changing; our location in it altering. In this chapter, I argue that being a Muslim in the emerging worlds—worlds unfolding into our futures—is both an ontological question and a proposition that requires a radical rethinking of the emotive and epistemic terms with which new regimes of knowledge might emerge and take shape. To cultivate a new language of grasping what it means to be a Muslim in this world requires an existential self-awareness. We need to cultivate that language in critical and caring conversation with the post-Western history in which we now live.

In our lived experiences of today we must overcome what is said and handed down in the language of "Islam and the West" before we can discover what it means to be a Muslim in the world. To achieve that end, first and foremost we need liberate ourselves from the received and coagulated *metaphors* in which we as a people have been trapped, and in which entrapment we are as much at fault as those who devised those traps for a sense of their own superiority and our domination. Those metaphorical traps are not conspiratorially manufactured. It is in the nature of all imperial imaginings to produce regimes of knowledge that rob their subject peoples of agency and decide even the terms of their revolts. We need to revolt in form, in style, in manner—and for that we need no guns or other weapons. Those who resort to violence have lost their way with forms. We need to articulate our agency in formal and epistemic conversation with a post-Western world unfolding right before our eyes. To be a Muslim in the world today is predicated on intuitions of *interiority*, marking a safe space from the politics of an ever-expansive *exteriority*—and these two adjacent spaces will have to corroborate each other. We might be a Muslim who prays five times a day, fasts during the month of Ramadan, pays his or her *Khums* and *Zakat*, performs her or his *Hajj* pilgrimage, has absolute certainty about our metaphysical origins and soteriological destination, and regulates his or her daily life on the strictest reading of our sacred law (in their multiple renditions). And yet we might be a Muslim who does none of those things and has alternative moods and manners (with or without historical antecedents among Muslims) of coming to terms with *the intuition of transcendence* in her or his innermost being. That condition of interiority is always

DOI: 10.1057/9781137301291

located in a manner of worldly exteriority that gives meaning and significance, solace and certainty, to a Muslim's metaphysical whereabouts. The oscillation between that interiority and the fact of that exteriority is as much an existential as a hermeneutic proposition. The dialectic of that interiority/exteriority I call "worldliness."

Can a Muslim ever arrive?

In one of those marvelous essays that it seems to me only John D. Caputo knows how to write, the distinguished American philosopher begins by playing footsie with Hans-Georg Gadamer and Jacque Derrida, in a gracefully choreographed move meant to learn (and to teach) "How to Prepare for the Coming of the Other."[4] I remember that when I was reading that essay, in the aftermath of 9/11, I quietly muttered to myself: "Well, I am a Muslim, of a sort, I live in New York City, and so I seem to be the other, right? And I have—all the indications testify to that effect—arrived. But have I arrived—can I ever arrive—here in New York, where I, after all, live, and where I call myself, willy-nilly, a Muslim?" How is one to prepare for coming of the other? Is not the other, as the other, the one for whom one is precisely not prepared? Does not the preparation relieve the other of his or her or its alterity so that, if we are prepared, then what comes is not the other but the same, just what we were expecting."[5] Fair question and an even fairer response, I thought to myself. But from which, were I not to conclude that I, as a Muslim—lapsed or lasting—can in fact never arrive, without my arrival being, for what it is, always announced, compromised, understood in terms already alien to me, by virtue of being familiar to my interpreter, alien to myself, my own Muslim self.

We Muslims (nominal or for real) all became Muhammad Atta on September 11, 2001. It made no difference what our names were—Muhammad, Ahmad, Hamid, Hany, Fatima, Mona, Lila, Najla, Golbarg, Maryam, Pardis, Kaveh, or Mahmoud. We all became, ipso facto, overnight, and without any say in the matter, "Muhammad," expected to respond to the question, "Why do they hate us? Why would they do something like that, Hamid," a colleague asked me on the morning of 9/11 on the Columbia University campus. The short pause, just before the sudden staccato of "Hamid," is where the issue rests. Why would I have any privileged access to the mind of a criminal who had just blown

DOI: 10.1057/9781137301291

up two beautiful towers in our city—except for the fact that the trilateral root of HMD connected my name to the name of a mass murderer? It never even occurred to me on April 19, 1995, when I heard about the Oklahoma City bombing, or later when I learned the names Timothy McVeigh, Terry Nichols, and Michael and Lori Fortier, to find a colleague and ask him, "Why would they do something like that," pausing for a meaningful moment before adding pointedly, "Tim, Nick, Mike, or Lori." But, why would this question not occur to me but would occur to any Tim, Nick, Mike, or Lori? There is the rub. We had indeed arrived—unannounced, unexpected, unwelcome—but had we, could we, ever? We, the other: precisely as John D. Caputo says—for "the West" could not possibly have waited or been prepared for us, to arrive, in that particular manner, crashing into buildings, maiming and murdering people—with no tongue, evidently, in our cheeks.

Professor Caputo credits Edmund Husserl's fifth *Cartesian Meditation* with having "marked off with great precision the *structural* non-knowing, the *structural* secrecy of the other person."[6] He then further clarifies that "the other whom I would know would not be other."[7] That seems perfectly sound to me. I must remain entirely confined to my own Muslim self—1.3 billion-plus of us reduced to one proverbial Muhammad Atta—for the radical hermeneutician to sustain his hermeneutic angst and pave his way to his, how does he put it, "radical hermeneutics." To be fair, "we Muslims" is not exactly what Caputo had in mind when spoke of "preparing for the coming of the other"—which absence is perhaps the best way of being and remaining an other. So, I thought to my own Muslim self, we as Muslims will have to remain the unknown, the mathematical X, like Malcolm X, the complete and completely alien *other* for the Husserlian philosophy to work. Right? For if we were to be known, assimilated backward and forward into the knowable world—to ourselves and to our own others—then both Husserl and Caputo, and along with them George W. Bush, Tony Blair, and Pope Benedict XVI will be denied their modus operandi of knowing things—just about anything—altogether. We are their blind spot, politically and philosophically, and by being their blind spot we enable them to philosophize and see things—*other* things to be sure, things *other* than us, for if they were to see us (their blind spots), then they would be blinded to the world at large, and that won't do, will it? It would be quite dangerous. They might get into an accident or something. In developing his "more radical hermeneutics," Caputo initially quite enthusiastically concurs

DOI: 10.1057/9781137301291

with Gadamer that hermeneutics is nothing other than putting one's own horizon playfully at risk, which proposition he then traces back to Heidegger's constitution of a *hermeneutics of facticity*, from which Caputo then concludes that hermeneutics is predicated on two poles—*facticity* and the *other*. From there Caputo continues to play on Gadamer's *analytics of finitude* and Derridian *différance*, paving his way toward what he rightly considers a more radical hermeneutics—in which the conclusion of the hermeneutic act is not getting to know who we (you, the reader, the interpreter, the hermeneutician) are but the recognition that we (you, the reader, the interpreter, the hermeneutician) in fact do not know who we are, or, alternatively, we do not discover what *the secret* is, but that the secret is that there is no secret. We may, as I did and as I habitually do, follow all that with admiration and even enthusiasm, and yet I and my own Muslim self were still wandering (loitering was more like it) between facticity and the other—and Caputo forgot (or just did not care, perhaps) to carry me and my humble Muslim self along with him to that finitude where I, too, can join him and say that yes indeed there is no you (I)—or that indeed there was no secret but the fact that there is no secret, for I was stuck with being *other*, or just integral to a *facticity* that needs and waits to be interpreted by Caputo's—now how in the world did he put it?—oh yes, "radical hermeneutics." I really wanted to be there, when Caputo discovered there was no secret. But alas, I was left behind.

So why would anyone—Muslim or otherwise—want to be the blind spot of other folks? The *other* that makes their *self*, even when they contemplate a radical hermeneutics, for which in your liminal space have deep appreciation and even admiration, even when they want to be so radical as to say that there is no secret or that there is not even a *you* or an *other* in the world—they still need you—the (Muslim) other, the quintessentially altered, neutered, othered, the Muslim, the Oriental—to be there *in negation* in order to be their blind spot so they can see better and discover how to be radical. There and then, even in the midst of a moment of a radical hermeneutics, you (the wretched Muslim) do not exist.

To be sure—and to be fair, for we ordinary Muslim folks cannot afford not being fair—Caputo did not have me or us Muslims in mind when he was theorizing this hermeneutic other of his, and perhaps precisely for that reason we Muslims remain his absolute and irreplaceable blind spot, the blindness that makes his insights possible.

So here we are, not only politically, but philosophically, hermeneutically, put in a very difficult spot, to be able to pronounce and confess

DOI: 10.1057/9781137301291

and declare we are a Muslim—entitled to an interiority, an exteriority, a worldliness. We are, as it were, there by virtue of not (being allowed) to be there. To be a Muslim in the world is an act of revolt against that hermeneutic annihilation.

The quiet America, the crowded Europe

In Spring 2011, I was invited by the University of Washington in St. Louis to give a series of talks to their faculty and students. While there I was invited by a kind Muslim physician and community activist to give a talk at a mosque he had helped establish in the city. After my talk at that Shi'i mosque, my host drove me to a much bigger, more opulent, Sunni mosque in the same vicinity. This mosque included a sizeable library and offered all sorts of community-oriented programs for those who attended it. Though I am honored to have been invited there, attending mosques in the United States or giving lectures in them is not my cup of tea. I grew up in mosques in my hometown in Ahvaz, and I have visited mosques across the Arab and Muslim world—from Morocco to Turkey, including the al-Aqsa' mosque in Jerusalem. But university campuses are my natural habitat, here in the United States and in Europe. The experience of visiting two Shi'i and Sunni mosques back to back in the middle of America (though they each welcomed the other's members) was not particularly remarkable except precisely in its nondescript habitat. From this suburban vantage point, it seemed that the overwhelming majority of Muslims in America lead calm, quiet, dignified lives—mostly under the radar of the loud and noisy outer America, of terrorism and the war on terrorism. This is not to minimize the larger Islamophobic battles Muslims from North America to Western Europe have to face. The combined banality of American neocons, belligerent Zionists, and Christian fundamentalists (aided and abetted by sorry comedians like Bill Maher) have made a metaphor of terror out of Muslims and their faith. Between these loud noises and quiet whispers, there is a calm, dignified America (where Muslims and most other Americans live) and a not-so-quiet and dignified America. Muslims are not exempt from this bifurcation. Alas, the world hears a great deal about the not-so-quiet and dignified America and its Muslims but precious little about that hidden side. In between these outer and middle Americas, Muslims can navigate between the possibilities of their interiorities and the fact of their

DOI: 10.1057/9781137301291

exteriorities, in which dwell the hermeneutics of alterity that must teach Muslims their renewed worldliness beyond the dead-end of even the most "radical hermeneutics" that an American philosopher can dream. Learning from this far more enabling hermeneutics of alterity, we may ask, how are Muslims *not* to fall into the trap of yet again playing second violin to the first violin of some binary opposition thrown their way—to become yet again the permanent other of someone else's self, who can never arrive? Islamophobia is only the façade of a European pathology of needing migrant labor but disliking migrant laborers, whereas in the United States, it has the added momentum of an ideologically provincial empire that lacks a convincing hegemony even to itself.

It is in these North American and Western European contexts that I make the case for a final break from such distorting, limiting, and exhausted frames of references as "Islam and the West." This rising and expansive Islamophobia, at times disguised or transfigured under the contorted politics of atheism, should not distract from the more urgent task at hand of learning the new language of being a Muslim in the world by inhabiting the emerging worldliness. The proposition necessitates a daring hermeneutic gesture. We must be careful not to allow this deeply racialized Islamophobia to determine the terms of our engagement with the world and distract us by entering into a detrimental dialogue with it. That forced political dialogue is constitutionally detrimental to any renewed conception of a Muslim sense of interiority.

Everything in that post-Western dialogue, or even the sheer possibility of that sense of interiority, depends on a full recognition of our renewed worldliness. The worldliness of the language means to be in the world, and this necessitates having a different interlocutor than "the West" and all its subterfuges. The mere sign "the West" means the death of interiority for anything that is "non-West." The worldly conversation that Gadamer theorizes in his hermeneutics "is a living process in which a community of life is lived out."[8] We must choose that "community of life" away from the racialized entrapments we face. We as Muslims in the world are living that life but do not yet speak its language. Gadamer's insight is paramount here: "Human language must be thought of as a special and unique living process in which, in linguistic communication, 'world' is disclosed."[9] What interlocutor we choose very much determines what world we will help create. In that world, where colonial and postcolonial boundaries in and out of Europe are shifting, the last thing European racist Islamophobes can claim is their

DOI: 10.1057/9781137301291

"national sovereignty" or "civilizational identity." Europeans lost their rights to their "national sovereignty" and "distinct culture" when *their* Christian missionaries went around the globe to Asia, Africa, and Latin America and taught the natives how to turn the other cheek when the colonial officers were slapping them in the face and burning them alive. Europeans forfeited their rights to their sovereignty when they went around the globe plundering one continent after another to build their "distinct culture." Europeans are the ones that crossed their borders to dominate, rule, plunder, and build their culture and industry. Crossing borders, stealing people's resources, and enslaving them has been definitive to *their culture.*

So when the late Oriana Fallaci in Italy and the retired Brigitte Bardot in France were aghast at the sight of Muslims and Africans in their streets and squares, they had simply forgotten the repressed truth of the civilization they believed was endangered. They only saw its pleasant and clean half (Via Veneto and Champs-Élysées) and repressed its ugly and ghastly half (sweat shops around the globe), which needed and needs to be better exposed for what it is. Oriana Fallaci's parental generation should have thought about the character of its national and European culture before it invaded, occupied, and plundered Libya. Brigitte Bardot's parental generation should have done the same when plundering the rest of Africa all the way to Asia. It is the morning after, the hangover of those drunken years. Now the inhabitants of those worlds are coming to Europe through the same gates that Christian missionaries and colonial officers going the other direction opened and crossed to rule, plunder, and enslave the world. They thought it was a one-way street. Alas: it is a two-way highway.

Muslims qua Muslims are integral to this world: their rich and fat princes and businessman are the beneficiaries of it. Their migrant laborers and illegal immigrants suffer the consequences of it. There is a fundamental and irreconcilable difference between the Islam of one and the Islam of the other. It is impossible to be a Muslim in between these two Islams without taking a stand, taking a side. The renewed *intuition of transcendence* for a Muslim in this world must begin in the basement of that restaurant where an Algerian illegal laborer is washing dishes and fearing the police. I have been to the Hassan II Mosque in Casablanca that the Moroccan monarch built. Indeed: it was majestic, but, alas, I searched it for God in vain. The cold, shivering, fearful, and soap-soaked hands of that illegal Algerian dishwasher—He is there.

DOI: 10.1057/9781137301291

Intentional blindness

In *The Myth of the State* (posthumously published in 1947), the eminent German philosopher Ernst Cassirer (1874–1945), thought through the proposition that the human mind and social actions are predicated on an early mythical phase that eventually works itself toward a rational reading of the world—thus trying to account for the rise of a fascism in Europe as a resuscitation of mythmaking.[10]Anti-Semitism was a dangerous myth in Europe then, as is Islamophobia now. The Anders Breivik massacre of innocent people in Norway on July 22, 2011, and the immediate Islamophobic reactions to it by the media and their "terrorism experts" were eerily similar to the reactions to the Oklahoma City bombing back in April 1995. Soon after the Norway massacre, video clips of American journalists, terrorism experts, opinion makers, politicians, and so on, resurfaced on the Internet—where they were caught with their hands in the cookie jar. On that day, being a Muslim, yet again, became an impossibility. For a few agonizing hours we were on the defensive, fearful that the yet-to-be-identified mass muderer might be a Muslim, relieved that he was not, at the same time angry that these people had rushed to think he was a Muslim—and in the midst of fear, relief, and anger, we had, already, lost our way as to how to be a Muslim, from the inner sanctum of our certainties rather than the circumstances of our being in the world. That being in the world—once again—had been made impossible.

In Norway a mass murderer left behind a manifesto in which he quotes and cites leading American and European neoconservative Zionists, pro-Israeli propaganda officers, and neo-Nazi organizations to justify his crime. Will anyone investigate these hatemongers for inciting murder? Thanks to the Norwegian authorities, we now have a complete document of the mass murderer's commentaries.[11]Will anyone look at the sorts of violent, Zionist, professional Islamophobes whom he favorably quotes and cites?

But beware: If we begin to ask these most obvious questions—the disabling terms of our being a Muslim in this world have already been determined by a handful of racists on the losing side of history. For as soon as we begin to ask them, we are trapped, for the reversed disease of anti-Semitism has already metamorphosed itself into Islamophobia, and militant Zionists have become its chief proponents (by a bizarre but perhaps perfectly understandable transmutation),and the ugly faces of

DOI: 10.1057/9781137301291

hatred, bigotry, and racism have transfigured our own moral and normative disposition into a reactive mode. To be a Muslim in the world,
we must run away from this disease—once we have carefully diagnosed
it—as from a plague.

Does anyone remember now the 12 writers who put their names on
a statement in French weekly newspaper *Charlie Hebdo* warning that
"[a]fter having overcome fascism, Nazism, and Stalinism, the world now
faces a new global totalitarian threat: Islamism."[12]They issued that statement right from the heart of Europe. It has been a while, so they may
have forgotten who they are. So who were the signatories? Ayaan Hirsi
Ali, Chahla Chafiq, Caroline Fourest, Bernard-Henri Levy, Irshad Manji,
Mehdi Mozaffari, Maryam Namazie, Taslima Nasreen, Salman Rushdie,
Antoine Sfeir, and Philippe Val, IbnWarraq. Would these ladies and gen-
tlemen care to issue a statement now—extending it to a mourning nation,
and perhaps acknowledging the role they played, however inadvertently,
in its national tragedy? Again: being a Muslim in the world is precisely
in the jeopardy of these thoughts even occurring to you—for by then
the native informers and the comprador intellectuals at the service of an
imperial hegemony have decided the terms of your self-consciousness.
They have won, you have lost: You are trapped. Beware!

The big elephant in the room

Societies and cultures that create Dinesh D'Souzas, Glen Becks, and book-
burning pastors, that can produce Geert Wilders and Niall Ferguson,
or that celebrate Ayaan Hirsi Ali and Ibn Warraq are in much need of
self-reflection. Every society and every culture has its sickness. Arabs and
Muslims have their own. Societies that have produced Osama bin Laden
and Ayman al-Zawahiri and Molla Omar, al-Qaeda, and the Taliban are
not healthy either. But look at the Arab and Muslim world from one
end to the other. It is arisen—against itself, against its habitual politics of
despair. People are revolting against tyrants that rule them, the banalities
that have infested their minds and souls, and the foreign dominations that
have kept them that way. Beyond the politics of despair, and the even more
debilitating politics of identity, of pitting one statistic of atrocities against
another—lies the vast highway of how to be a Muslim in the world.

The Norwegian massacre is ultimately a European issue. Europe has
a choice: It will either go the predominantly BBC way, which found a

grief stricken Norwegian calling the mass murder "insane," or it will go the way of *Guardian,* which published an absolutely brilliant essay by Matthew Goodwin, arguing that "Breivik is not a Norwegian oddity, but symptomatic of a growing culture of politically motivated violence across Europe."[13] But Muslims should not do what Islamophobe Europeans did to them. This is the time to refrain from the terrorizing term "Christian terrorist." We must remember the fear and trembling our parents as new immigrants felt when they heard the term: Muslim terrorists. There are millions upon millions of pious and good Christians round the globe. Breivik is an aberration to their faith. The ability to liberate ourselves from the fangs of Islamophobia and think in solidarity with Christians who share his faith but not his murderous deeds is the first step toward being a Muslim in the world. Perfectly decent, highly educated, widely traveled Europeans honestly believe, without the slightest sense of irony, that it was "simply a numbers game" that led reasonable people to assume Muslims had committed the atrocity in Norway, for in recent years Islamists have been responsible for innumerably more plots against the West and for slaughtering random people. The fact that "in recent years" a vastly higher number of innocent Muslims have been slaughtered by European and American troops in Afghanistan and Iraq, and by the Israeli apartheid state in Palestine and Lebanon, with the weaponry that they provide, entirely escapes them when they talk about a "numbers game." For every innocent American killed by Muslim terrorists (which is one too many), at least a thousand innocent Afghan and Iraqis have been murdered. For every one innocent Israeli that has been murdered by suicidal violence (which is one too many), at least one hundred innocent Palestinians have been murdered. Point blank. And yet these perfectly decent, perfectly rational, logical, deeply learned, and widely traveled Europeans say that "the numbers game" goes to their side. This is the power of metaphor—isolate statistics in one area; disregard them in the rest of the world. No Muslim ever voted for Osama or the Taliban. But these Europeans and Americans voted for Blair and Bush and Berlusconi—and yet what these daddies do at work is irrelevant to these children at home. Whether Breivik is "[a]right-wing Christian fundamentalist who may have had an issue with Norway's multi-cultural society," as CNN described him,[14] or simply a right-wing racist bigot who, like his kindred souls in Europe and United States, hates both the progressive Left and Muslim immigrants, goes on a rampage killing dozens of mostly teenagers at a summer camp on an island in

DOI: 10.1057/9781137301291

Norway—the cerebral, instinctive, reaction of European and American journalists, columnists, anchorpersons, radio talk-show hosts, and the "terrorist experts" they fished out of a Philadelphia or Washington DC think tank and invited on their shows was that it was a Muslim terrorist act. Why? Based on official statements by Norwegian authorities, and the manifesto that the accused mass murderer self-published, the world now has a fairly accurate picture of who he is, what he believes in and why he did what he did. "Anders Behring Breivik, the man accused of the murder of at least 92 [Norwegian authorities later reduced the number to 76] Norwegians in a bomb and gun massacre," the *Guardian* reported,[15] "boasted online about his discussions with the far-right English Defense League and other anti-Islamic European organisations." These were the emerging facts, but the metaphors had already done their work. It mattered not that he had blonde hair and blue eyes, and was a born and bred Norwegian who does in fact hate Islam and Muslims. One terrorism expert said to a television anchorwoman after this information became known, "we never know, this could be a disguise." Further investigations revealed[16] that the suspect was a member of a Swedish neo-Nazi Internet forum called Nordisk. He believed that "Muslims are trying to 'colonize' Western Europe and that he blames multiculturalism and 'cultural Marxism' for permitting this." He also believed that "there is not one country where Muslims have peacefully lived with non-Muslims, stating that instead it has had 'catastrophic consequences' for non-Muslims." In short, the accused mass murderer was not only not a Muslim, he was a Muslim hater, and that hatred, plus his hatred of the Left, was the motive behind his mass murdering of people in a government building and at a youth camp run by a political party he holds responsible for having allowed undesirable elements into his Norway. But these are only the unworthy, pedestrian, facts—they pale in comparison to the might and majesty of the reigning metaphors.

Muslims as metaphors

Even more gruesome details emerged in a 12-minute anti-Muslim video called "Knights Templar 2083" in which images of Mr. Breivik appear. The BBC reported that "a Twitter account attributed to the suspect has also emerged but it only has one post, which is a quote from philosopher John Stuart Mill: 'One person with a belief is equal to the force of 100,000

DOI: 10.1057/9781137301291

who have only interests." The Norwegian newspaper *Verdens Gang* also quoted a friend of Breivik who said that "the suspect turned to right-wing extremism in his late 20s." That is, 12 years ago, a couple of years before 9/11. Breivik's manifesto, called "2083: A European Declaration of Independence," minutely elaborates the author's belief that a process of "Islamisation" is under way. Mr. Breivik was previously a member of the right-wing Progress Party (FrP), the second largest party in Norway's parliament. He became a member in 1999 and paid his last membership fee in 2004. He was deleted from the member registry in 2006. Poor facts—the foot soldiers of an already waged and lost battle—were marching in. Why is it that otherwise respectable people and news organizations wishing to establish their credibility cannot wait a mere 24 hours for all the official reports to come out? And if the demands of the round-the-clock news cycle are so urgent that they must be fed continuously, why do the news outlets immediately suspect Muslims? Whence the power of these metaphors: Islam and Muslims as evil incarnate? The world of course is no longer at the mercy of the *New York Times*, the *Financial Times*, the BBC, or any other news conglomerate. Within hours after misinformation from major news outlets began to circulate, Shiva Balaghi had written an article for *Jadaliyya* exposing the horrid rashness of the press, and showing that they had jumped their guns in naming Islamic terrorism as the culprit, advising: "In this 24/7 news cycle driven even more mad by terror experts who conduct research using google and tweet a mile a minute, journalists should exercise caution."[17] Soon, Juan Cole was also on their case, giving journalists a statistics lesson: "Europol reports have long made it clear that the biggest threat of terrorism in Europe comes from separatist movements, then from the fringe left, then from the far right. In 2008, only one terrorist attack out of hundreds in Europe was committed by radical Muslims. In 2010, according to Europol, seven persons were killed in terrorist attacks. Some 160 of these attacks that year were carried out by separatists. The number launched by people of Muslim heritage? 3."[18]

Soon after, Glenn Greenwald was even more relentless in making a case for the banality that passes for journalism in North America and Western Europe: "For much of the day yesterday [July 22, 2011], the featured headline on the *New York Times* online front page strongly suggested that Muslims were responsible for the attacks on Oslo; that led to definitive statements on the BBC and elsewhere that Muslims were the culprits. The *Washington Post*'s Jennifer Rubin wrote a whole

DOI: 10.1057/9781137301291

column based on the assertion that Muslims were responsible.[19] Jennifer Ruben, a pro/Israeli blogger who started at the *Jerusalem Post* and is now bringing her vast experience as a journalist to a chain of New York pro/Israeli tabloids and to a blog for the *Washington Post*, was among the first to divine—following a lead by the beacon of neoconservative chicanery and the loudest mouth in Israeli propaganda machinery in the United States, the *Weekly Standard*—a link between "Jihadists" and the Norway terror attack. As Glenn Greenwald rightly detects, even in President Obama's statement there was the hint of a suggestion that Muslim terrorists were involved." The morning statement issued by President Obama—"It's a reminder that the entire international community holds a stake in preventing this kind of terror from occurring" and "we have to work cooperatively together both on intelligence and in terms of prevention of these kinds of horrible attacks"—appeared to assume, though (to its credit) did not overtly state, that the perpetrator was an international terrorist group.[20] Greenwald is very generous with the president; he doesn't ask what phrases like "the entire international community" or the even more pointed reference to working together "in terms of prevention" might mean. President Obama and Jennifer Rubin were on the same page. Glenn Greenwald's major point, however, was something else:

> But now it turns out that the alleged perpetrator wasn't from an international Muslim extremist group at all, but was rather a right-wing Norwegian nationalist with a history of anti-Muslim commentary and an affection for Muslim-hating blogs such as Pam Geller's Atlas Shrugged, Daniel Pipes, and Robert Spencer's Jihad Watch. Despite that, The New York Times is still working hard to pin some form of blame, even ultimate blame, on Muslim radicals.[21]

Jennifer Rubin, President Obama, and the entire editorial staff of the *New York Times* were working from a simple repertoire of metaphoric identification: Muslims were terrorists; terrorists were Muslims. The two terms have become interchangeable, redundant. The people that Glenn Greenwald names have been instrumental over the last decade or two in making sure that when people hear the word "Muslim" they hear "terrorist"; and when they hear "terrorist" they hear "Muslim."

The *Wall Street Journal* called Breivik an "al-Qaeda copycat." This is precisely the function of a metaphor. If even Martians start to confuse the terms, they will have done it based on the model, the blueprint, of

DOI: 10.1057/9781137301291

the metaphor. So what's wrong with the immediate gut reaction being that this act, too, was perpetrated by Muslims? This is in fact precisely what Jeffrey Goldberg of *The Atlantic* argued in defense of Jennifer Rubin's early divination, stating, "It is not perverse or absurd for normal people to think of al Qaeda when they hear of acts of mass terrorism. It is logical, in fact, to suspect al Qaeda. The Norway catastrophe does not negate the fact that the majority of large-scale terrorism spectaculars by non-state actors over the past decade have been committed by Muslims."[22] There are quite a number of nuggets in this very sentence I will let go for now to make another point. The gist of the argument is that they have done it before—so maybe they have done it again. What's wrong with suggesting that? Statistics be damned, Muslim terrorists are capable of doing it and they might have done it—right? The problem with a metaphor is that you cannot discuss or debate it, analyze or rebut it. You cannot refer to history, to cause and effect—who has done more terrorizing acts of violence to whom—Israelis to Palestinians or Palestinians to Israelis, Americans to Iraqis or Iraqis to Americans? You cannot subject a metaphor to facts, figures, statistics, causality, counter narratives, or the enormity of what Americans have done in Afghanistan or in Iraq or Israelis in Palestine or Lebanon—compared to the acts of violence that all Muslim terrorists put together have done. Metaphor is cerebral. It has nothing to do with facts, defies reason, commands reaction, compliance, response. People like Jeffrey Goldberg or Jennifer Rubin can act like they own the world, for they speak and write from behind the shoulder of the American marine and the Israeli colonial officer roaming the globe or the region to claim and control it. They thrive on metaphors. It is their business, their careers. Our problem is that if we allow them to decide the terms of engagement with our world at large, they have already won the game.

In fact, what we see in Europe and North America is not "Islamophobia," for a "phobia" is a deeply rooted fear of uncertain or repressed origins. It is a deliberately and consciously manufactured loathing systematically cultivated by right-wing extremists, many of them active members of the Zionists propaganda machine operating from Tel Aviv to New York. Conditioned by pro-Israeli propaganda that has systematically sought to demonize Islam and Muslims, it is in fact the transmutation of an entire people into a metaphor. This is not a conspiracy. It is a case of a very limited number of tropes, metaphors, and allegories, categorically hanging on those interchangeable terms "Muslims" and "terrorists."

DOI: 10.1057/9781137301291

The only thing that counters a metaphor is a counter-metaphor. The counter-metaphor of Muslims as terrorists is called "the Green Movement," "the Jasmine Revolution," or "the Arab Spring." Arabs and Muslims have finally broken free of from their postcolonial fate, as millions have poured into the streets demanding that their regimes—not just their political regime but the regime du savoir that had coupled them to "the West"— be overthrown.

Muslims and the Left

Consider the following titles: *Unholy Alliance: Radical Islam and the American Left* (2004) by David Horowitz; *The Enemy at Home: The Cultural Left and Its Responsibility for 9/11* (2007) by Dinesh D'Souza; and *The Grand Jihad: How Islam and the Left Sabotage America* (2010) by Andrew C. McCarthy. The list of such titles is long. Hold your nose and look them up on the Internet, on Amazon, on websites that pop up like unseemly mushrooms, or else just visit your local bookstore. They are usually on the bestsellers desk. Phrases fulminate: "the modern left and Islamic fascism," "unholy alliance of Islam and leftists," "exposing liberal lies: the odd marriage between Islam and the Left." It is quite an industry: books, articles, websites, blogs, tweeters, think tanks, white supremacists, native informers, comprador intellectuals, terrorist experts, entrenched Zionists, neoconservatives for hire. The message is simple: The Left and the Islamists have come together to destroy Western civilization, beginning with its first and final defense line, the good land of Israel. One of the grandest charlatans among them published a book he called *The Professors: The 101 Most Dangerous Academics in America* (2006)—I am one of them—in which he lists the leading American academics who are either characterized as Left or profiled as Muslim. This "Left" has become a generic term, a sponge-word. It includes feminists, gay activists, and scholars, as well as activists and scholars in the fields of African American studies or race and ethnic studies, whatever the white, masculinist imagination wishes "multiculturalism" to mean—all the undesirable elements, in short, populating the nightmares of the authors who write those books, the publishers who publish them, the people who actually pay money to buy these books and read them. Watch Zach Snyder's movie "300" (2007): All the creatures in Xerxes' army, well, they are the visual summation of "Muslims and the Left." Evidently there is

DOI: 10.1057/9781137301291

a lucrative market for this kind of gibberish in the United States. And where there is demand there is supply—the simple logic of capitalism.

Look at just one of these bestselling authors—Dinesh D'Souza. Look at the title of some of his books: *What's So Great about Christianity; What's So Great about America; Ronald Reagan: How an Ordinary Man Became an Extraordinary Leader; Life after Death: The Evidence.* The man has one simple idea: his notion of America and his version of Christianity are the greatest things that ever happened to humanity, and everything else, the Left and Islam in particular, are the darkest evils that ever were, condemned to hell unless, like him, they see the light, join his church, and get saved. He loves an abstraction he calls "America," which to him is a white America, but, and here is the rub, he is not white. The man is a dark-skin Indian. But he seems to see himself as a white warrior of Greek mythology in Zach Snyder's movie. Muslims and the Left, gays and blacks, feminists, and multiculturalists—these are the creatures he sees in front of him, his nightmares. D'Souza used to be in the company of like-minded people at the conservative Hoover Institute in California. He is now the president of his own college, responsible for the education of an entire generation of students.

But D'Souza is not alone. He is a *New York Times* bestselling author, as they say. Thus prominent editors seek him out, offer him lucrative contracts, and publish him with pomp and ceremony. His books are sold, read, discussed, and reviewed in print and electronic media, on the basis of which he then gets invitations to give public lectures and interviews. The cycle is self-perpetuating, endless, implicating an entire industry, not just one person and his perhaps outlandish ideas. Vintage D'Souza: "The cultural left in this country [USA] is responsible for causing 9/11... the cultural left and its allies in Congress, the media, Hollywood, the non-profit sector and the universities are the primary cause of the volcano of anger toward America that is erupting from the Islamic world."[23] The cultural left and Islam: put together, with their allies in government, media... responsible for acts of terrorism. Does that ring a Norwegian bell? There is an entire industry catering to precisely the sort of "insanity" with which the Norwegian mass murderer is afflicted—an industry that banks on people fusing the Left and Muslim and seeing the result as the supreme metaphor of menace to civilized life.

This fusion of the Muslim and the Left—as if a Muslim cannot be on the Left, or a person on the Left a Muslim—brings together the historic American fear of the Left and its newly minted fear of the Muslim.

DOI: 10.1057/9781137301291

The result is the aggressive transmutation of the Muslim into a classic metaphor of fearful fantasy, devoid of historicity, exteriority, interiority, worldliness.

The larger picture

American slang is filled with racial slurs that reflect contempt for people at the receiving end of North American military invasions and conquests: Commie, Brownie, Buffie, Camel Jockey, Chinaman, Chinky, Coolie, Darkie, Gooky, and soon after the US-led invasion of Iraq, *Haji*, referring to any Iraqi or Arab in or out of sight of American GIs. These derogatory terms are used to distance and denigrate the people they were fighting, subjugating, conquering. They are dehumanizing terms that turn "the enemy" into a "thing" so that he can be dispensed with—with a clear conscience. Since the 1950s and the McCarthy witch-hunt, the Left has been made into the America's nightmare by the Right. The Left is a fifth column. If the Soviet Union was the enemy without, the Left was the enemy within, wanting to sabotage the system to further the cause of the enemy without—the same way that the US Catholics were accused of being more loyal to the Pope in Rome than to the American constitution—and the way that now Muslims are considered the enemy within. Arthur Miller in *The Crucible* (1953) went all the way back to the Salem, Massachusetts, witch trials of 1692 to diagnose the pathological fear that had engulfed Americans in the 1950s during the so-called Red Scare: the First (1919–1920) and the Second (1947–1957) Red Scare. Today, the identification of the Left with the Muslim is straight out of the genre of the witch-hunt. What Dinesh D'Souza and the whole platoon of less talented but more pestiferous old and new conservatives he represents have been doing over the last few decades in the United States is to help transfuse the fear and loathing of the Left onto the fear and loathing of Muslims—and they have succeeded. This transmutation of the Left and the Muslims into each other is a recent development that predates 9/11 and began in earnest soon after the Hostage Crisis of 1979–1980.A key contributing factor of course has been the Israeli propaganda machinery that has succeeded in persuading Americans that (facts be damned) all Palestinians are Muslims, all Muslims are terrorists, and that Israel is really fighting for Americans in the frontline of defense against barbarity. That in his "Clash of Civilization" thesis, Samuel Huntington, a chief

DOI: 10.1057/9781137301291

theorist of American imperialism, perceived Islam as the civilizational enemy number one of "the West" is a key summit point in this transmutation. The practice is straight out of German Nazi political philosopher Karl Schmitt (1888–1985)—without an enemy there is no concept of the political. The very concept of the political is predicated on the existence (fabrication) of an enemy. A combined hatred of the Left and of Muslims (being a black/Latino radical Muslim gay is really the full Sunday Best regalia here) informs a wide range of public commentary in the United States that goes far beyond Dinesh D'Souza and Samuel Huntington and has employed a whole regiment of less intellectually gifted but nevertheless quite verbose characters. These two neoconservative icons are just symptomatic of a much more widespread syndrome.

What we are witnessing in this transfusion of the Left and the Muslim, however, is only one critical element in the constitution of the Muslim as a menacing metaphor. The systemic machination behind the demonization of Muslims as a menace to humanity is not limited to a neoconservative and Zionist operation. When it comes to Muslims as the epitome of evil, the list in fact swings all the way from the Right to the Left. The anxiety motivating the identification of the Muslim with the Left is the anxiety of the enemy within. But when we catch the Left itself using the Muslim as a metaphor of banality and terror we are onto something far deeper in the inner anxiety of the thing that calls itself "the West." Consider this phrase: "He is a caliph, I suppose, almost of the Middle Eastern variety." This is Robert Fisk, the distinguished British journalist, probably furthest in his political disposition from Dinesh D'Souza and Samuel Huntington and their ilk—and this is the opening sentence of an article he wrote on July 11,2011, for the *Independent* in which he shared his thoughts on Mr. Rupert Murdoch at the height of the UK phone hacking scandal.[24]Why that curious opening—why a "caliph," of all things, of "the Middle Eastern variety?" What other variety of caliphs do we have, anyway? Scandinavian caliphs? Australian? British? There is only one kind of caliph. The word comes from the Arabic *Khalifa*, meaning a representative, a vicegerent. It was first used in its historic meaning in the aftermath of Prophet Muhammad's death in 632 CE, when Abu Bakr, his comrade, succeeded him. Abu Bakr and his supporters opted for the humble title of "representative of the Prophet of God," not wishing to pretend they were equal to him. Other successors of the prophet followed suit, calling themselves "caliph," until finally, the first and second Arab dynasties of the Umayyads (661–750) and

DOI: 10.1057/9781137301291

the Abbasids (750–1258) were formed, and they called their institution a "caliphate." Other dynasties such as the Ottomans (1299–1923) also at times used that title. Now, were some of these caliphs (as any other monarch or queen or caesar or pope) corrupt, authoritarian, wealthy, and such? Of course they were. But why when it comes to a metaphor of corruption, banality, and tyranny, can Mr. Fisk not think of one from his own backyard: popes, caesars, British monarchs, perhaps "Bloody Mary," Il Duce, Mein Führers? Why Middle Eastern caliphs when referring to Rupert Murdoch, AC, KSG, the Australian-American global media baron—that AC officially coming after his name standing for The Order of Australia, an order of chivalry established by Elizabeth II, Queen of Australia, and that KSC being The Pontifical Equestrian Order of St. Gregory the Great (Ordo Sancti Gregorii Magni) established by Pope Gregory XVI in 1831? There are plenty of metaphors to work with from Mr. Fisk's own neighborhood in all of that. Why could Robert Fisk not "suppose" any of these real things and reach for "almost" something else other than a "Middle Eastern" metaphor? But it is not just Robert Fisk. The syndrome is an epidemic. The Muslim is a metaphor of menace, banality, and terror everywhere—from the Right all the way to the Left. Here is another prominent example. Lewis H. Lapham, the distinguished former editor of *Harper's Magazine*, a singularly progressive, left-leaning American critic of US imperialism, too, does not hesitate for a minute to invoke Islamic metaphors when he wants to denigrate and dismiss his conservative opponents. In a critical review of David Frum and Richard Perle's horrid book, *An End to Evil: How to Win the War on Terror* (2003), Lapham unabashedly ridicules Frum and Perle for having borrowed their inspirations from "the verses of the Koran," for issuing "fatwas" like Osama bin Laden, and for summoning "all loyal and true Americans to the glory of jihad"—all the while calling them "Mullah Frum," "Mufti Perle," or "the two Washington ayatollahs," concluding: "Provide them [Frum and Perle] with a beard, a turban, and a copy of the Koran, and I expect that they wouldn't have much trouble stoning to death a woman discovered in adultery with a cameraman from CBS News."[25] If Lapham needs to invoke the best metaphor for an unquotable propaganda prose, he cannot think of a better example than the Qur'an, nor does he pause for a moment to think through the implications of what he says:

> As with all forms of propaganda, the prose style [of Frum and Perle's book] doesn't warrant extensive quotation, but I don't do the authors a disservice by

DOI: 10.1057/9781137301291

reducing their message to a series of divine commandments. Like Muhammad
bringing the word of Allah to the widow Khadija and the well Zem-Zem, they
aspire to a tone of voice appropriate to a book of Revelation.[26]

If Lapham needs an appropriate allegory for indoctrinating hatred, and
terror, Islam and the Qur'anic language are handy:

> *The result of their* [Frum and Perle's] *collaboration is an ugly harangue that if*
> *translated into Arabic and reconfigured with a few changes of word and emphasis*
> *(the objects of fear and loathing identified as America and Israel in place of Saudi*
> *Arabia and the United Nations) might serve as a lesson taught to a class of eager*
> *jihadis at a madrasa in Kandahar.*[27]

Examples abound and are not limited to *Harper's Magazine*. The pages of
The Nation, another left-liberal periodical in the United States, are replete
with derogatory references to conservative adversaries, again using
Islamic metaphors: mullahs, madrasah, turbans, verses from the Qur'an,
and so on. Terry Jones, the Florida pastor who burned the Quran is an
easy target—he is just a simple man with honestly racist views wear-
ing his bigoted heart on his sleeves. People with a far superior claim
to progressive, liberal, left, and tolerant ideals have been at work here
sustaining "the Muslim" as a metaphor of evil for a very long time. Here
is Maureen Dowd, an open-minded liberal columnist for the *New York
Times*, criticizing the Republican vice-presidential nominee Paul Ryan:

> Unlike some of the right-wing ayatollahs, Ryan doesn't threaten with moral
> and cultural gusts of sulfur. He seems more like a friendly guidance coun-
> selor who wants to teach us how to live, get us in shape, PowerPoint away
> the social safety net to make the less advantaged more self-reliant, as he
> makes the rich richer. Burning the village it takes to save it, so we can avoid
> the fiscal cliff, or as he and his fellow conservative Cassandras ominously
> call it, "the debt bomb."[28]

The possibility of a *"right-wing rabbis"* or *"right-wing bishops"* is not an
option here. The issue here is not catching these journalists red-handed.
The issue is how Muslims became the dominant metaphor for menace,
terror, and mendacity. In thinking through that transmutation, it
is clear that an even larger frame of reference is at work. It is not just
Europeans or Americans, and it is not just the Left or the Right, that use
and abuse Islamic terms freely as metaphors of dismissal and denigration, vilification and disparagement. The practice is predicated on the
more fundamental binary opposition established between "Islam and
the West." The binary has been manufactured, corroborated, and driven

DOI: 10.1057/9781137301291

home by no other Orientalist, dead or alive, more adamantly, more dog-
gedly, more persistently than Bernard Lewis. But every time a Muslim
or Arab scholar, journalist, activist, public intellectual uncritically uses
the delusional term "the West"—"the West did that" or "the West will do
the other thing"—she or he is corroborating that binary between "Islam
and the West. It makes no difference if you say, as Dinesh D'Souza or
Niall Ferguson do, that "the West" is God's grandest gift to humanity;
or, reversing that, say that "the West" is the source of all horror in the
world. In either case you are corroborating the a/moral authenticity of a
reference that ipso facto posits and negates "Islam."

As manufactured in "the West," in the battle of metaphors between
"Islam and the West," "the West" is good, "Islam" is bad. "The West" is
cowboys, "Islam" the Indians. As an Arab or a Muslim you may reverse
the order, but you will only exacerbate the binary opposition, the delusion that clouds reality. Arabs and Muslims are as much at fault for cross-
authenticating "the West" and positing it as the primary frame of moral
reference, within which Islam and Muslims are staged as metaphors of
evil and banality. Where the Left and the Right come together is thus
in the constitution of Muslim as *the civilizational other*, the ontological
alterity, of the sand castle that must call itself "the West" or else it will
doubt and dissolve itself back into the shadow of its own nullity. In seeing
through this epistemic free-play of signs, it is not sufficient, necessary,
or even advisable to go back to the European history of Orientalism, to
Dante's *Divine Comedy* (1308–1321) or Mozart's *The Abduction from the
Seraglio* (1782), or even as far back as Aeschylus' *Persian* (472 BC) on a
goose chase after the origin of "the Oriental" and later its rendition as
"the Muslim" as the supreme other of "the West." There was no "West" at
the time of Aeschylus or even Dante—and the Orientalism of each one
of these eras differs from the other. That kind of historicism dilutes the
issue and confuses the focal point of *iteration* through which the delusion of "the West" keeps repeating in order to keep believing in itself. We
need surgical precision as to how and when and for what purpose the
figure of the Muslim is posited as the supreme metaphor of menace—for
instant, knee-jerk reaction. Who benefits from this spontaneity, what
invokes it and to what effect, and with what barefaced persistence? Yes
indeed, the constitution of Muslim as a metaphor of mendacity and
menace to civility and society is predicated on older tropes. But today
it is the handiwork of North American, Western European, and Israeli
journalism (three specific sites for three specific reasons), and as such

DOI: 10.1057/9781137301291

it is now exposed for the hideous lesion that it is on the body politics of a constitutionally flawed narrative that has perpetrated unfathomable terror on generations of Muslim children and their parents around the globe, frightening them out of their wits that there is something constitutionally wrong with who and what they are. The world is no longer at the mercy of this corrupt cacophony of power and wealth. They have analyzed and terrorized us enough. It is time to get even, expose and theorize them back.

To be a Muslim in this world

To be a Muslim in the world begins with placing ourselves outside the metaphoric matrix onto which we have been, willy-nilly, cast, unbeknownst to ourselves. That "selves" in the "ourselves" is already worldly, placed on a matrix of global self-awareness that must become actively conscious. Over the last two hundred years, we have been metamorphosed into metaphors of other people's narratives, narratives of fixed disposition and evidently irreversible grammatology. We need to conjugate ourselves out of that grammar. Those metaphors are the tropes of imperial imaginings beyond our control, having in fact taken control of us. Those imaginings posit an Osama bin Laden and an Ayaan Hirsi Ali and invite (indeed command) us to opt for one of them. To be a Muslim in the world begins with refusing to be part of that game—to say the hell with both of them. To defy that fake option, instrumental in the making of an imperial imaginary that has no room for any person—any self or other—is the first step toward being Muslim in *this* world. To be a Muslim in the word means to own up to all the horrid crimes perpetrated en masse not just in the name of Islam but by other Muslims, by the ruling regime of the Islamic Republic, or the criminal banality of the Taliban or al-Qaeda, of the mass murders perpetrated in Mumbai, Madrid, or New York. They are done not just in the name of Islam but by perfectly legitimate Muslims. Just because there is a turgid Islamophobia on the European and American continents, it does not mean Muslims do not need to do some serious soul-searching. Any religion that has created a mass murderer like Osama bin Laden and a charlatan like Ayaan Hirsi Ali of course needs to do some serious soul-searching, not on the terms set by Thomas Friedman, or Bernard Lewis, or Dinesh D'Souza but decided by Muslims themselves. The renewed terms of that

DOI: 10.1057/9781137301291

soul-searching are and will determine the moral contours of the next generation of Muslims, their sense of interiority, their place in the world, and their cultivated intuition of transcendence.

Notes

1   Max Weber, *The Sociology of Religion*. Translated by Ephraim Fischoff, with an introduction by Talcott Parsons (Boston: Beacon Press, 1922/1956): 1.

2   Ibid.

3   Ibid: 262.

4   See John D. Caputo, *More Radical Hermeneutics* (Bloomington: Indiana University Press, 2000): 41.

5   Ibid.

6   Ibid: 41.

7   Ibid.

8   Gadamer, *Truth and Method* (op. cit.): 404.

9   Ibid.

10   See Ernst Cassirer, *The Myth of the State* (New Haven, CT: Yale University Press, 1961).

11   See "Anders Behring Breivikskommentarer hos Document. no." Available at http://www.document.no/anders-behring-breivik/. Accessed June 21, 2012.

12   See "Writers Issue Cartoon Row Warning." (BBC, March 1,2006). Available at http://www.bbc.co.uk/news/world/asia/.Accessed June 22, 2012.

13   See Matthew Goodwin, "Norway attacks: we can no longer ignore the far-right threat" (*The Guardian*, July 24, 2011). Available athttp://www.guardian.co.uk/commentisfree/2011/jul/24/norway-bombing-attack-far-right. Accessed June 23, 2012.

14   See:http://articles.cnn.com/2011-07-23/world/norway.suspect_1_youth-camp-norway-nrk?_s=PM:WORLD.

15   See http://www.guardian.co.uk/world/2011/jul/23/norway-attacks-utoya-gunman.

16   See http://www.bbc.co.uk/news/world-europe-14259989.

17   See: http://www.jadaliyya.com/pages/index/2202/tragic-day-for-norway;-shameful-day-for-journalism.

18   See:http://www.juancole.com/2011/07/white-terrorism-in-norway.html.

19   See: http://www.salon.com/2011/07/23/nyt_17/.

20   Ibid.

21   Ibid.

22   See: http://www.theatlantic.com/international/archive/2011/07/on-suspecting-al-qaeda-in-the-norway-attacks-updated/242416/.

DOI: 10.1057/9781137301291

23 See: http://www.dineshdsouza.com/books/the-enemy-at-home-the-cultural-left-and-its-responsibility-for-911/.

24 See: http://www.independent.co.uk/news/media/press/robert-fisk-why-i-had-to-leave-the-times-2311569.html.

25 See: http://harpers.org/archive/2004/03/0079930.

26 Ibid.

27 Ibid.

28 See:http://www.nytimes.com/2012/08/15/opinion/dowd-when-cruelty-is-cute.html?_r=1&hp.

DOI: 10.1057/9781137301291

5

Din, Dowlat and *Donya*: Rethinking Worldliness

Abstract: *In Chapter 5, I ask how the terms "religion" and "state" be separated—what does it mean to ask for a secular politics, divorced from people's sacred certitudes? By analyzing three Arabic/Persian words:* din *(religion),* dowlat *(state), and* donya *(world), I raise the linguistic horizon we need to revisit as we come ashore to a new globality of our consciousness.*

Dabashi, Hamid. *Being a Muslim in the World.*
New York: Palgrave Macmillan, 2013. DOI:
10.1057/9781137301291.

DOI: 10.1057/9781137301291

My friend and colleague Professor Ahmad Sadri called for a conference titled "Future of Secularism and the Public Role of Religion in Post-Islamist Iran" at Illinois's Lake Forest College, where he teaches. It was March 2010, less than a year after the June 2009 post-electoral crisis in Iran, and in an eerie yet revealing way my friend's invitation was reminiscent of that of Jürgen Habermas, who in 1979 had called for a similar conference of leading German intellectuals to reflect on "The Spiritual Situation of the Age."[1] Were we in Lake Forest to reflect on the "spiritual situation" of our age, of our world, too, perhaps?

When Habermas invited prominent German intellectuals to reflect on the spiritual situation of the age, he threw a monkey wrench at them. He asked them to take Karl Jaspers's 1931 essay *Die Geistige Situation der Zeit* as their point of departure. So their reflections had an immediate double meaning; guests would be reflecting, not just on the spiritual situation of the age, but also on Karl Jaspers's seminal and prophetic essay. Ahmad Sadri did no such thing. He was probably too polite to limit his guests to any specific terms. But the sense of urgency informing his call for critical reflection in 2010 was in fact far more acute than what had prompted Habermas in 1979.

Habermas and other German intellectuals were concerned, first and foremost, about the transmutation of their homeland into a battleground between the two superpowers. But with an uncanny premonition of what would happen 30 years later in Iran and prompt Ahmad Sadri's call for a conference, German intellectuals were equally concerned with and beholden to the rise of a Green Movement in Germany, *die Grünen*, as it was called. The German Greens, as Andrew Bushwalker reminisces, included not just environmentalists, but also "urban squatters, feminists, counter-cultural youth, and members of an increasingly influential peace movement."[2] This generation of Germans, too, was branded "post-materialist" and "post-acquisitive," in much the same way their Iranian counterparts at the time of the Lake Forest gathering were being considered "post-ideological."

The nature of the crisis

These similarities notwithstanding, Ahmad Sadri and those he invited to Lake Forest were deeply concerned about much graver and more brutal, even existential, issues. They were all headed for Lake Forest at a

DOI: 10.1057/9781137301291

time when the custodians of the Islamic Republic were kidnapping their brothers and sisters off the streets of their homeland, throwing them into their dungeons, torturing them and reportedly even raping and murdering them and burying them in unmarked graves or parading them on national television to humiliate them into confessing to outlandish charges. Nearly all the invited guests who had come to Lake Forest were persona non grata in their homeland, and the notorious dungeons of Kahrizak or Evin would be their first destination if they ever dared to return to Iran. A brand new pair of prison pajamas awaited them, along with television cameras, Kangaroo courts, and already typed-up and ready-to-be-signed confessions that they had all been fooled by the misbegotten ideas of Max Weber, Jürgen Habermas, and Richard Rorty, assured by the "authorities" that George Soros had opened a personal bank account for them on the condition that they believed sultanism was the real nature of the Islamic Republic.[3]

As we gathered in Lake Forest, it was not just the atrocities of the intelligence, security, military, judiciary, and clerical apparatus of the Islamist regime that was pulling asunder the moral and normative fabric of our homeland. The very territorial integrity of that homeland, the threat of crippling economic sanctions, covert operations, and military strikes—endangering the lives and livelihood of millions of Iranians—hung in balance. The situation would get even worse with the passing years. But the hope that the Green Movement had generated in June 2009 was the anxiety underlying our fear in that fateful March in 2010.

There was also an abiding sense of moral crisis that governed the spirit of the age at the time that Ahmad Sadri called on his friends and colleagues to gather in Lake Forest. The Islamic Republic had banked heavily on and callously invested the ancestral faith of a people—their sense of sanity, sanctity, and solace, their pride of place as a people, as a nation entitled to a name, the dignity of a *mellat*, a metaphysical sense of point and purpose to who and what they are, of their origin and destination, the *Mabda'* and the *Ma'ad* of their worldly and otherworldly whereabouts. The Islamic Republic of Iran had kidnapped their intuition of the sacred. That intuition had to be recultivated from the ground up (for the time of the vertical descent of the sacred was long since over)—but how, upon what common grounds?

What would happen to Islam and to Muslims in Iran after an Islamic republic? Would it be possible, and if so on what terms, for Iranians to remain or call themselves Muslims after an Islamic republic or a fortiori

DOI: 10.1057/9781137301291

after the torture and reported rape in dungeons of Kahrizak? In his "Elahiyat-e Shekanjah" ("Theology of Torture") Mohammad Reza Nikfar, a leading Iranian dissident intellectual based in Germany, had taken not just the Islamic Republic, but Islam itself, in fact, God Almighty himself, to task and implicated the Qur'anic transcendence in the moment of torture and rape in the dungeons of the Islamic Republic.[4]Mohsen Kadivar, a prominent oppositional Shi'i cleric based in the United Sates, did not like this equation or consider it fair. But fair or not—the question and the equation Nikfar had posited revealed the pain of a people, not over the torture and possible rape, but for having their sense of sanity and solace beaten and raped out of their innermost sanctities by their own brothers and fathers. There was and is something maliciously incestuous about the rape of our children by the militant thugs in the dungeons of the Islamic Republic. Had the parents of these children risen up in revolt against a tyrannous monarchy 30 years ago so that our children could be raped, tortured, and murdered in an Islamic republic? Mohammad Reza Nikfar had put his accusatory finger on a gushing wound and would not let go; and as a principled and courageous cleric, Mohsen Kadivar had difficulty turning his face from the scene of crimes that implicate not just the Islamic Republic he opposes but also the Islam he is sworn to defend. How exactly is a Shi'i cleric to defend Islam under these circumstances—by positing an *Islam-eRahmani* (a benevolent Islam)?But where was that Islam-eRahmani when children were being summarily kidnapped from their streets and homes and frightened out of their wits, their faith? Nikfar was relentless, Kadivar was defensive. The question was irresoluble in the terms they kept exchanging.[5]

The moral crisis of the Islamic Republic occurred at the time of a global purgatory, where and when the binary of "Islam and the West," too, had effectively lost its navigational compass. If in 1979 Habermas had inaugurated the gathering of German intellectuals with an homage to Karl Jaspers's essay "The Spiritual Situation of the Age," in 1931 Jaspers had been invoking the articulation of the Hegelian *Geist* in *Phänomenologie des Geistes* (1807) and its subsequent thematic unfolding in history and historiography. Though Ahmad Sadri stipulated no similar frame, his invited guests had gathered in Lake Forest at a time of a post-Hegelian "end of history" proposition, when a bureaucratic functionary at the US Department of State had in the late 1980s declared the time of the world at its thither end.[6]Less than a year after the commencement of the Green Movement in Iran, and before the rise of the Arab Spring, the rebirth

DOI: 10.1057/9781137301291

of history was yet to become a common trope on the global scene. So the question remained at once urgent and yet limited at the time of the conference, but it would soon explode onto the global scene when the participants returned home to await on a global scale what they had only sensed in the Green Movement.

Before those world historic events were to unfold, Francis Fukuyama had summoned his Hegelian spirit (through the intermediary of his teachers Alan Bloom at Cornell and Samuel Huntington at Harvard, and of their teachers Leo Straus and Alexander Kojève) forgetting his Karl Schmitt and the conceptual necessity of an Enemy for the political virtues of neo-conservatism and neo-liberalism to shine forth and enlighten the humanity under the torch of US imperialism. But soon his teacher Samuel Huntington, in his *Clash of Civilization,* recognized the folly of forgetting that indispensable Enemy, and instantly posited Islam and thus Muslims as its most recent incarnation. Early in the 1990s, not too long after the end of Reagan's "Evil Empire," we saw the rise of George W. Bush's "Axis of Evil"—the political brainchild of the Project for a New American Century that had brought Fukuyama together with the most notorious yuppie warmongers of the United States, a trajectory of opportunism that from the Hoover Institution in California to SAIPS in Washington DC boasted one native informer after another as bicoastal bookends of the compradorial opportunism this brave new world had to offer. Between the demise of the "Evil Empire" and the rise of the "Axis of Evil" Christian and Christological soteriology remained at the heart of this most Christian empire, with Jewish Zionists and Muslim native informers in full attendance.

Theories travel, as the late Edward Said used to say,[7] and thus we were there in Lake Forest also under the shadow of the goodhearted "Smiling Seyyed" (Seyyed-e Khandan), the former President Mohammad Khatami who had heard about Samuel Huntington's idea of "the clash of civilizations" and proposed in return a "dialogue among civilization[s]." Evidently no one had told the good president that (1) Huntington's principal target was the home front of the all-white America facing massive labor migrations from the darker continents that were threatening "Western Christianity," a concern as far back as sixteenth century, when Bartolomé de las Casas and Juan Ginés de Sepúlveda were debating how best to keep the Americas Christian; and (2) that Huntington had created his own "Islam," yet again, as the civilizational other of "the West," creating an enemy precisely to generate Schmittian fascist virtues, and certainly not to invite them to a dialogue.

DOI: 10.1057/9781137301291

The Muselmann

But by the time Samuel Huntington and President Mohammad Khatami were exchanging banalities and pleasantries alike, Giorgio Agamben was busy writing *Homo Sacer* (1998) and *Remnants of Auschwitz* (1999).[8] In *Homo Sacer,* Agamben revealed how the concentration camp (from Auschwitz and Buchenwald, which he used as examples, to Sabra and Shatila, which he did not) has become "the nomos of the earth," and as such the best example of the Foucauldian biopolitical domain. In *Remnants of Auschwitz,* he advanced that political diagnosis to the point of moral crisis, when it is the political that decides and administers "the life worth living."

Agamben had borrowed from Benjamin, Arendt, and Foucault to posit his notion of "homo sacer"—but this was no mere theoretical stipulation, and in fact, it uncovers the Italian philosopher's blind spot. That both Hannah Arendt in 1951, the year her *Origin of Totalitarianism* was published, and Agamben in 1999, the year the English translation of the *Remnants of Auschwitz* appeared, had almost exclusively in mind the figure of the German Jewish refugee, never pausing to consider the Palestinian refugee as a variation on the same theme, reveals much, not just about their philosophical insights, but about their moral and political blinders as well—blinders that can only be lifted by taking Levinas's phenomenological alterity of the face of the other at its philosophical face value, disregarding Levinas's own moral and theoretical short comings in not facing up to the implications of his own philosophy and acknowledging Jewish culpability for Sabra and Shatila. In this regard, Arendt, Levinas, and Agamben were all on the same page as Golda Meir: for them Palestinians (the subaltern of the subaltern) did not exist!

But the blotted-out figure of the Palestinian refugee is not the only inadvertent object of Agamben's insight; such is the fate of the young Iranian demonstrators who were kidnapped and taken to Kahrizak. Mirroring her or his Palestinian brothers and sisters in Gaza, the Iranian Muslim child being molested, raped, tortured, and cold-bloodedly murdered in Kahrizak was the simulacrum of the figure of the *Muselmann* in the German concentration camp. As used at the camps, the term *Muselmann* (Muslim) meant a passive inmate who had completely given up hope on life, had neither a mind nor a soul, who had become, literally, a walking dead person, a homo sacer, "despised and...a mere staggering corpse, a bundle of physicality of no consequence."[9]

DOI: 10.1057/9781137301291

The similar fates of the young Iranian demonstrators and their Palestinian brothers and sisters assimilates "the garrison state" (Harold Lasswell's 1941 term), from the Islamic Republic to the Palestinian refugee camps, and both become the textual analogues of Hannah Arendt and Giorgio Agamben's European insight—though they are too European to see that they are in fact theorizing the Palestinian refugees. The similarity, however, is not in the degree or intensity of brutality in one camp or another, but (as Agamben rightly notes) in the stripping of the incarcerated person's civic identity and the baring of that identity to broken bone and the shed blood.

By yet another serendipity, 1979, the year of Habermas' meeting, was also the year of the Iranian revolution—and 30 years later, Habermas himself stood accused of plotting a velvet revolution to topple the Islamic Republic. Thirty years earlier, the political crisis of a tyrannical monarchy had yielded to the rise and the exacerbated moral crisis of an even more tyrannous Islamic Republic. When Shah collapsed, monarchy, we were told, was thrown into the dustbin of history. Thirty years later, what exactly was to be thrown into the selfsame dustbin? The moral malady, political banality, and the spiritual corruption of an Islamic republic? What had to survive that historic inevitability were what Muslims called Islam, the holy text they called the Qur'an, and the sense of the sacred and certitude and the intuition of transcendence that hold and uphold the moral mandates of a people together. Could Muslims survive having become a *Muselmann* in the dungeons of an Islamic republic?

Karl Jaspers' essay came out of the Germanic tradition of anti-modernity that ranged from Oswald Spengler and Martin Heidegger to Ferdinand Tönnies and Carl Schmitt, and then went west to Spain to include Ortega y Gasset.[10]It was one such German anti-modernist, Ernst Jünger (1895–1898), whose 1950 classic *Über die Linie* had reached Jalal Al-e Ahmad (1923–1969) via Ahmad Fardid (1909–1994),ultimately resulting in his notorious notion of *Gharbzadegi,* "Westoxication"(1962), the cornerstone of the eventual Islamist takeover of the polyvocal Iranian political discourse in the 1960s, which ultimately resulted in the violent over-Islamization of the 1979 revolution. Dariush Ashuri's famous critique of Al-e Ahmad's *Gharbzadegi*, and his subsequent fanatical devotion to "the West" and to "modernity" as the panacea for all our ills, not only did not correct the course, but in fact deepened and exacerbated the spurious and misbegotten binary that ultimately resulted in the equally outlandish storm in the teacup of Aramesh Dustdar and his

DOI: 10.1057/9781137301291

notion of *Imtena' Tafakkordar Farhang-e Dini* ("Impossibility of Thinking in a Religious Culture"). Dustdaris Al-e Ahmad's *Gharbzadegi* in a mirror, or its *doppelgänger* (the ghostly double), to be more precise. Jalal Al-e Ahmad and Aramesh Dustdar are flipsides of the same coin—the violent alienation of creative thinking in two diametrically opposed directions, both effectively distorting the factual evidence of a worldly cosmopolitanism of all Muslims, Iranian or otherwise.

Between Jalal Al-e Ahmad and by extension Ali Shari'ati on one side and Dariush Ashuri and Aramesh Dustdar(and all their followers)on the other was sustained the colonially crafted and false binary between "Islam and the West," or "tradition versus modernity," and all their other conceptual mutations such as "self and the other," "familiar and the foreign," that to this day plague the Iranian intellectual disposition and political discourse. Just as Al-e Ahmad and his company saw the disaster we face as having come from "the West," Ashuri and his clan saw the panacea of all ills coming from the selfsame fictitious source. Between the two camps they corroborated a false consciousness they termed "the West." If Al-e Ahmad, and after him Shari'ati, sent their admirers and followers on the goose chase of a "return to the self," Ashuri's company and its colonized mind instigated a deep sense of self-denigration and self-alienation. The two pathologies continue corroborating and confirming each other.

Of course, neither Al-e Ahmad nor Ashuri invented either "Islam" or "the West"—as bone of contention or as binary. Colonized minds, one in a defiant and the other in a compliant way, they were simply partaking in an act of civilizational self-othering definitive to European Enlightenment modernity. Instead of seeing the condition of coloniality as the abuse of labor by capital writ geographically large, and not indulging in a deeply racialized identity politics, they went for the constitution of the spatial bordering of capital as a reality sui generis. Iranian intellectuals were of course not the only players in this false field—not even its best players. The selfsame distortion happens in the Aimé Césaire/Frantz Fanon constitution of *negritude* or even in Jose Marti's conception of *our America*—all articulated beyond class and gender. Neither Tayeb Salih nor Albert Memmi, in *Season of Migration to the North* (1966) and *Pillars of Salt* (1953), respectively, could resolve the dichotomy in which Al-e Ahmad and Ashuri were trapped and in which they had trapped an entire political culture and its captured audience. But Memmi's Benillouche Alexandre Mordekhai at least had the wisdom

DOI: 10.1057/9781137301291

of leaving horizontally (metaphorically) for Argentina (neither East nor West), instead of becoming a criminal like Tayeb Salih's Mustafa Saeed. Saeed would of course re-emerge in English literature as V. S. Naipaul, the self-loathing Oriental who in *A Bend of the River* (1979) recreated both himself and his literary antecedent in the figure of Salim. None of them—from Jalal Al-Ahmad to Mustafa Saeed, from V. S. Naipaul to Dariush Ashuri—had the globality of vision that made W. E. B. Dubois's expansive authenticity and Malcolm X's explosive revolutionary authenticity predicated on their defiant cultural inauthenticity. It is only in the presence of W. E. Dubois's monumental and transcending intellect that all these figures can be seen for what they are.

The same way that the anti-modern strain in the German philosophical disposition of the 1930s ultimately resulted in the frenzied terror of Hitler, with Martin Heidegger, Karl Schmitt, and other German anti-modernists joining the Nazis, the anti-modern legacy of Jalal Al-e Ahmad and his disciples culminated in the charismatic terror of Ayatollah Khomeini and the formation, in the aftermath of the cultural revolution, of the category of "religious intellectuals" and the purging of the universities, actions that it instigated and later disowned.

The constitution of "the West" became integral to a binary in which Islam became "Islamism," and the twain of "Islam and the West" not only constantly met but in fact copulated and begat religious intellectuals on one side and secular intellectuals on the other—twin brothers and Cain and Abel to each other's negation. "Islam and the West," "tradition and modernity," "religious and secular" began chasing after their own tails, and in the vertiginous spinning, the machinery of the Islamic Republic sustained itself. In other words, in its most recent vintage, the battle between Nikfar and Kadivar reproduces this binary anew, and as such is not only not outside the ideological killing machine of the Islamic Republic—it is in fact definitive of its epistemic modus operandi, for they are reenacting Ashuri/Al-e Ahmad for the next generation. But despite this similarity, Nikfar's criticism remains far closer to the moral crisis of the Islamic Republic, while Kadivar's positions stay entirely oblivious to that debilitating crisis, which after Kahrizak needs a far more serious critical encounter with the juridical scholasticism he seeks to update for a post-Islamic Republic era.

Habermas's 1979 call to action to reassess "the spiritual situation of the age" had of course a therapeutic dimension in assuaging the post-Holocaust German angst. But Ahmad Sadri's invitation to Lake Forest

DOI: 10.1057/9781137301291

was bracketed between and in the shadow of two university purges in the Islamic Republic that would have made a gathering like this in Tehran impossible—one that had marked the commencement of the Islamic Republic in 1979 and the one that had just marked its moral demise in 2009. The university purges in the Islamic Republic were identical to the Nuremberg Laws of 1935 in which the Nazis declared Jews non-Germans and forced scores of prominent German Jewish intellectuals like Adorno into exile. Kamran Daneshju, the persistently falsifying, plagiarist, and arsonist minister of higher education in the Islamic Republic had plainly threatened that any university campus that did not comply with his estimation of an Islamic education he would raze to the ground.[11]

Along with many other German academics and intellectuals, Adorno left Germany, first for Oxford and subsequently for the United States, where he lived a traumatic exilic life fearing for his parents (until they too fled Germany for Switzerland) and broken by the suicide of his friend Walter Benjamin. Unlike many other observers of the horrors of European Holocaust, Adorno did not see the catastrophe as an aberration but as the natural outcome of the European Enlightenment, of instrumental reason, of administered life, and the transmutation of humans to things—a fact and phenomenon definitive of the colonial edges of European modernity but hidden and denied in Europe until the Holocaust. It did not even occur to Adorno, or to any other German or European intellectual that his justifiable horror at the European Holocaust was nowhere in sight when the selfsame Europeans were doing the same and worse to Asians, Africans, and Latin Americans throughout the colonized world. But those who were administering university purges in Tehran, Shiraz, or any other university and forcing non-Islamist scholars into prisons, retirement, exile, or oblivion were all in the extended shadow of the selfsame logic of the Enlightenment modernity that had the Holocaust at one of its ends and the nativist or the Islamist or modernist or any other sort at the other. But the abiding wisdom of Adorno now also teaches us that the catastrophe we now face as an Islamic Republic is not an aberration but is in fact the natural outcome of the violent over-Islamization of our polyvocal culture that commenced when the leading religious intellectuals were appointed by Ayatollah Khomeini to purge Iranian universities of non-Islamist elements. In the aftermath of the Green Movement in June 2009, Ayatollah Khamenei ordered that the work that generations of religious intellectuals had left unfinished be completed. Kamran Daneshju did

DOI: 10.1057/9781137301291

not appear out of nowhere. You need to ask yourself: who was Kamran Daneshju of 1979?

But there is nothing more boring and useless than a vindictive historiography. We, all of us, face a much more urgent task. Because the university purges from 1979 to 2009 were not only an ideological task but an infinitely more important key component of the stripping of *citizenship* to *bare life*, where students and faculty became the simulacrum of the citizen and were subjected to the ideological whims of an increasingly garrison state. Trespassing *the naked life*—stripped of *bios* down to *zoë*, of *civil* down to *human* rights—means coming to terms with the transmutation of Tehran into a garrison, the Tehran University campus into a camp, and Kahrizak into the simulacrum of Auschwitz, and above all, with the fact that the juridical-political system that calls itself an Islamic republic has transformed itself into a "killing machine," for here the *auctoritas* and *potestas* have collided in the ValiFaqih. In that active, historic, transmutation, it is no longer sufficient for Mohsen Kadivar to oppose Velayat-Faqih, or posit a fictive *Islam-e Rahmani* for the real militant Islamism that rules his homeland and from which he has run away to the United States. For now the entire juridical machinery he is trying to update is in fact under erasure, as Nikfar rightly sensed and suggested.

Saving "the naked life" (Agamben's pointed language) is to restore its civic protections against the killing machine, and that will not happen unless Islam is decoupled from the forced binary that has embedded and invested it in its own alterity, or the alterity of its own making. What was lost between "Islam and the West," between "tradition and modernity," "the religious and the secular" (or now, between the *din*, "religion," that was now presumed immaterial and sanctimonious and *dowlat*, "state," that was forced to be disambiguated and made secular) was *donya*—the "world," and above all, the worldliness, and is precisely here that Nikfar's militant secularism is equally, if not more, flawed.

The insufficiency of separating din from dowlat

At the time of the transmutation of the nation-state into camp, *bios* into *zoë*, civil rights into human rights, human into Musselman, Muslim into Taliban, the United States Constitution into the Patriot Act and Homeland Security Act, and ipso facto of *citizen* into *naked life*, it is not just *din* but equally so *dowlat* that are the modus operandi of the

DOI: 10.1057/9781137301291

biopower and governmentality. The globalized explosion of metastasized techniques of the subjecting, subjection, and subjugations of bodies and minds are far too advanced a condition of the naked life, and far beyond the outdated debate over whether the Islamic Republic is a nineteenth-century Weberian-sultanism or a mid-twentieth-century Lasswellian garrison state, to wake up from the nightmare of the Islamic Republic and its Velayat-e Faqih to an eighteenth-century dream of separating din from dowlat. Something far more immediate is at stake.

The gathering storm to separate din from dowlat at the dawn of the twenty-first century and the appearance of the naked life, though a very precious eighteenth-century Enlightenment relic, will have absolutely no consequence whatsoever on protecting our naked lives at a time when our naked bodies are the final site of the biopower that calls itself an Islamic Republic, on the trail of a nightmare in which Bush, Blair, Bin Laden, and Berlusconi had seen to it (and the Islamic Republic was on the same plane of reference) that pre-emptive strike and pre-emptive and indefinite incarceration have radically altered both the spirit and the mind, body and soul, of this particular age.

Keep in mind that Agamben's post-9/11 insight on the naked life was predicated on Arendt and Benjamin's post-Holocaust recognition of the selfsame phenomenon. So somewhere between the Jewish Holocaust in mid-twentieth-century Europe and the surfacing of the Bagram Airbase, Abu Ghraib, and Guantanamo Bay in the far corners of the US empire early in the twenty-first century, nation-states (both in their din and in their dowlat) degenerated into camps, and their citizens into bare lives. I have deliberately stated this in patently European terms to underline the fact that this whole separation of din and dowlat business (or Church and State, to be exact) is a European phenomenon at the capital end of Enlightenment modernity. For if I were to move (as I habitually do) to the colonial end of the selfsame modernity, where as a colonial and an Oriental I dwell, I would really not need the Jewish Holocaust or European philosophers from Benjamin and Arendt to Foucault and Agamben to tell me that my body—the body of the African, Asian, and Latin American de-subjection of European subjections—has been naked from the get go in this business they call "modernity," when at the height of its instrumental criminality, where the German juridico-political machinery had become a killing machine (Agamben's frightful phrasing), they called their dead men/women walking, their zombies, their bare lives by my name—a *Muselmann*, a Muslim.

DOI: 10.1057/9781137301291

So at this particular moment, when Guy Debord's "Society of Spectacle" has become the foregrounding of iconic violence of either the 9/11 sort or the "shock and awe" of the Donald Rumsfeld vintage, asking for separation of *din* and *dowlat* at the dawn of the twenty-first century is similar to administrating *Khakshir* and *Sonbolatib* (old-fashioned herbal medicine), though perfectly delightful concoctions, to a patient suffering from multiple sclerosis, psychotic schizophrenia and manic-depressive disorder. It is not just the Islamic *Republic* in which Kahrizak is now the locus classicus of Velayat-e Faqih, but Islam itself that has become coterminous with the globalized atomization of bare life; it is not just the *Islamic* Republic where the broken bones of Mohsen Ruholamini (a young man tortured to death by the security forces of the Islamic Republic during the rise of the Green Movement) have become the ground zero of the bare and brutalized life, but the aggressive transmutation of any republic into the state of exception, that threatens and overwhelms the naked life. So our twenty-first-century solution for the calamity of the Islamic Republic cannot be a naïve, simple-minded, and outright ludicrous eighteenth-century European relic of the Enlightenment in which we say that din and dowlat ought to be separated. This no longer is the issue—the calamity is far more advanced, the response needs to be far more radical.

Inserting donya: the world between din and dowlat

What if—here is *my* point of contention—in the binary opposition posited between din and dowlat, we were to interject the worldly wisdom of *donya*(the world), and thereby dismantled the more frightful metaphysical binary of din and donya on the side of a reading of Geist that is more *worldly* than *spiritual*. What if in between the binary opposition of din and dowlat we were to interject the worldly wisdom of the world, of donya, or, to put it differently, the effective history of our lived polyvocal experiences, and thereby dismantled the binary altogether on the side of a reading of *Geist* that as the Hegelian *Weltgeist* is far more worldly than spiritual? That is my contention.

Here is where a hermeneutic of unforeseen consequences can be seen suggesting itself. What if the far more critical "spiritual" crisis of our time, the time of *Kahrizak*, in contrast to the more innocuous *geistige Situation der Zeit* of both Jaspers and Habermas, before and after Auschwitz, were to be read through the employment of *time* by and into

DOI: 10.1057/9781137301291

the *world*—*Zeit* by and into *Welt, Zaman* into *Jahan*? What if we were to take the Hegelian notion of *Geist* in his *Phänomenologie des Geistes* as he posited it on the hook of the *Weltgeist*? *Geist* for Hegel was always contingent either on a *Weltgeist* or on a *Folkgeist*. So "the world" and the people who world it are the tertiary space where the old, tired, clichéd, and useless binary between din and dowlat absolve, resolve, and once and for all discredit and discharge themselves. The question is not the fact that din and dowlat must be separated—they must. The question is that the apposition is a camouflage, a smoke screen, a distraction from the more important and critical question of the opposition between din and donya to be once and for all absolved. Din and donya must embrace each other far more urgently than din and dowlat must let each other go. Put more emphatically, if din and donya were to embrace each other din and dowlat will let each other go.

In disciplinary terms, and in manners of new knowledge production, and in honoring Ayatollah Ali Khamenei's naming of sociology as the principal cause of his troubles and woes, what if we were to take Ahmad Sadri's *Max Weber's Sociology of Intellectuals* (1994) as our clue and point of departure. Imagine that we are to begin with a renewed pact with *Geisteswissenschaften*, not as "spiritual sciences," which would be meaningless, but as the domain of the humanities (*Olum-e Ensani*) in the nineteenth-century German idealist tradition. Wilhelm thought of the emerging discipline of sociology as *Geisteswissenschaften*, as did Max Weber and Edmund Husserl. So *Geist* here would not be read as *Spirit*, but as *Spirit of the world*, or simply *the world*, or what Hans Georg Gadamer called "effective history," or Edward Said, "worldliness," or what in Persian we would call *donya* or *donya'i*.

The naked life that this active worlding of the world is to cover is the pre-monitory Robert Musil's *Man without Qualities* (1930–1942), the self that has not entered any society, the slave-pariah that invokes Malcolm X's childhood and Ralph Ellison's invisible man, from which emerges Richard Wright's *Native Son*, when criminality, or self-criminalization, to be more exact, becomes the first modus operandi of selfhood, that would be Malcolm X in Boston as pimp and drug pusher. Malcolm X's conversion to Islam is when the man becomes a person, a Muslim, a Black Muslim, a double negative in the white supremacist context of its articulation, and thus twice a man, a person, a personhood, engulfed and protected not by a generic religion but in fact by *the palpable world* he has crafted around himself.

DOI: 10.1057/9781137301291

In my manner of suggesting this worlding of the world, inhabiting it with inhibitive particularities that mark the otherwise uncharted universe as ours, with a sense of belonging and possessing that defines the contours of citizenship. The binary between din and dowlat, for religion and state, will then be exposed as ipso facto unstable and thus irrelevant not just because "state" is supposed to be stable and dowlat (from DWL) keeps spinning around its own tail, but because they, as binary, at one and the same time, both inhabit and inhibit the notion that makes them possible, namely, the donya that they wish to control will turn around and embrace them. In other words, dwelling on the binary din-dowlat will yield the donya to their individual and mutual control, whereas our concern, pre-occupation, and primacy must be in having them yield their abused history to the grace and care of donya. Both din and dowlat have an innate and ipso facto claim to permanence, whereas donya by definition is *donya-ye fani*(fragile world). The fragility of the *fani* is, I believe, where we need to hang the impermanence of our life and the permanence of *shahrvandi*(citizenry) that must once and for all become the most irreducible building block of our once and future republic.

I, in other words, mean to override the binary of din and dowlat with the abiding worldliness of the donya that they must, ipso facto, inhabit and inhibit at one and the same time. The *Geist* as spiritual that keeps pulling the din and the *political* as power that keeps pushing the dowlat are effusively lost in the belligerence of their own, while the donya that sustains them demands but does not exact the worldliness that sustains them. Din and dowlat, in this reading, dissolve into donya and from that dissolution emerges the infinitely more abiding republican citizenry that neither denies nor privileges din as the binary of dowlat. It simply absolves them of their originary authenticity in positing civil liberties of a citizen within a republic as the political moment of our liberation.

Suppose we were to revisit the Hegelian *Geist* and read it not simply as the Spirit but as *Weltgeist*, as the Spirit that unfolds in and by world history, and thus as world history, or simply as the unfolded world, or even more simply as the world, the way Gadamer considered the world as the product of effective history and the horizon of all acts of interpretation. The metaphysics contingent on this worldliness is neither secular nor sacred. It is worldly, tertiary, supplementary, to the binary of both, and thus tangential to their belligerent differences. The supplementary interjection of donya is the Derridian "dangerous supplement" that supplants the cozy binary that din and dowlat have negotiated for themselves by

DOI: 10.1057/9781137301291

pretending to be at odds with each other. Donya notes and acknowledges din-dowlat binary for their *jang-e zargari* (fake feud) with a "whatever"— the way American teenagers use the phrase to both acknowledge and dismiss the seriousness of a matter.

Donya, fragile, is the abode of hope and happiness twined with fear and trembling, where Kierkegaard hung his faithful doubts and taught the world its hidden hopes. Upon a sea of such hidden hopes, fear and trembling is the defining moment of this event we call the Green Movement, for after all, we had all gathered there at Lake Forest in the shadow of Kahrizak, where our children were incarcerated, tortured, reportedly even raped, and murdered. I tremble in the distant shadow of Kahrizak. I fear, and I dwell on my fear. I envy Mohammad Reza Nikfar who has a God to blame for this torture. I envy Mohsen Kadivar who has a God to defend against this torture. I on the other hand dwell on my fear and trembling, frightened by the moment, precisely at the moment when my children are told to take off their pants, or their pants are torn off of their frightened and fragile limbs. I wish I had a torturing God to blame; I wish I had an innocent God to defend. But I am blinded by fright—by the moment when a club is inserted into the innermost sanctity of a human soul through a hole in her or his broken body. It is that broken body that must be the site of a bodily resurrection in this world, the one we live. The fright—as we have known it from Victor Eremita, the editor of *Either/Or* to Anti-Climacus, the author of *The Sickness Unto Death* and *Practice in Christianity*—is where the worldly dwells.

I wish thus to purpose the idea of *worldliness, donya'i*, as a take between Gadamer's mapping of the "effective history" and Edward Said's critique of imaginative geography (foreign facts becoming familiar fictions, to paraphrase him), and where *the world* becomes the domain of not just the material but also the abode of the metaphysical, and where Muslims matter more than Islam.

The colonial modernity of the opposition posited between the sacred and the secular updates the medieval bifurcation between donya and *akherat*, where *the transient world* is trapped in the former and the *intransient sacred* claims the latter. As a typical medieval example, Khwajah Nasir al-Din Tusi in *Akhlaq-e Muhtashami* (composed circa 1232) devotes one whole chapter (Chapter 15) to "Denouncing the World"("Fi Madhamah al-Donya"), and yet another full chapter (Chapter 16) to "Turning Away from the World and Embracing the Hereafter."My festive idea of donya celebrates what Tusi and the entire medieval Persian

DOI: 10.1057/9781137301291

andarz literature mourn—from Omar Khayyam to Forough Farrokhzad dwell in this permanent celebration of the impermanent donya.

Restoration of a fragile principality to donya, a retrieval of the world as the locus classicus of an impermanence that makes all metaphysics of permanence possible, works towards a reclaiming of a material metaphysics, the way it is posited in Abbas Kiarostami's factitious cinema and Mohsen Namjoo's improvisational frivolity alike, or—to show its premodern origins—somewhere in between Rumi's paradisial height and Sa'di's worldly wisdom, where Hafez has managed (for all of us) to love and to mourn worldliness at the same time.

If the fusion of din and dowlat has lent the metaphysical permanence of one to the political impermanence of the other—and in the course of our despotic history has given us the *Zill Allah fi al-Ard*, the *Aryamehr*, and now the *ValiFaqih*—their desired and enviable separation will have to fear and preempt the material vacuity of one (dowlat) replacing the immaterial metaphysics of the other (din). In other words, out of the frying pan of Aryamehr we have been dropped into the fire of Vali Faqih, two successive metaphysics of power—an Iranian and an Islamic (Shi'i). In order not to repeat the vicious circle, we need to get out of it, and allow for the failing binary of din and dowlat to be dissolved in the factual impermanence of a fragile, vulnerable, and thus trustworthy world. Neither din nor dowlat can or should be trusted—they are too metaphysical in their dead certainties. Only the vulnerable fragility of an impermanent world can guarantee the permanence of our civil liberties.

Instead of the dissociation of din and dowlat we need to dissolve them into donya—so in fact, instead of a post-Islamist or post-secular society, whatever those descriptors may mean, I am in effect arguing for a pre-Islamist and pre-secular society where (noting Talal Assad's genealogical recognition of both as tropes in the making of colonial modernity) the historical uses and abuses of both have indeed done their damage and have exhausted themselves.

In other words, if we allow donya to supplement din *versus* dowlat and through a Derridian supplementarity let it supplant the cozy arrangement disguised in the evident hostility between din and dowlat, we will have once and for all overcome the debilitating binary and ask them to pack their belongings and leave our language. To shift the theoretical lens to a different register, but making the same point, the mediating space of *worldly remissive* (I am extrapolating from Philip Rieff's theory of the sacred and its return as the return of the repressed), will allow for

DOI: 10.1057/9781137301291

the transgressive and the interdictory to have a more pliable adjudication, altogether overcoming the binary of the sacred and the secular. This shift I propose quintessential in the cultivating of a renewed intuition of the sacred within this world and beyond the institutions of power such the Shi'i clerical establishment that have laid an exclusive claim on "religion."

The employment of din and dowlat in the material immanence (self-fulfillment) of donya is where that necessary separation will preempt the imminent possibility that the dismantling of one metaphysics at Kahrizak does not yield to the construction of another licensed by the disenchantment of the word—where the not-so-hidden violent metaphysics of the secular has grabbed the not-so-different violence of the religious by the throat and does not let go.

The dissolution of din and dowlat into donya will restore to din its endemic heteroglossia that the monologue soliloquy of Fiqh with itself is as much responsible for overriding that polyvocality, as is the antinomy between sacred and the secular. Whereas this fabricated antinomy between din and dowlat is imported into the system, that heteroglossia is natural to its habitat. The absolutist nomocentricity of Islamic law has never been singularly definitive to its historical and worldly disposition. It is only in conversation with colonial modernity that this absolutism of Fiqh triumphed over (by scaring away) its equally legitimate discursive nemesis. If we were to restore the cosmopolitan character and polyvocal chords of our anti-colonial modernity to its pre-Islamist disposition, as it were, so will the cosmopolitan heteroglossia of Islam in its worldly habitat be more compatible with the emerging donya in which Muslims find themselves. The Islam that we know today and that is hidden under the political transcendence of Islamism is the product of colonial modernity with which Muslims began to define their place-in-the world. It is not post-Islamism that we need to have, but the pre-modern heteroglossia of Islam retrieved via a post-modern intimacy with fragile agency, with a mimetic crisis that resolves itself always momentarily.

The donya I thus posit is the modus operandi of recasting the moral and epistemic map of the globe, for the passage to institutionalization of democracy needs to be an act of spontaneous decolonization too. Militant secularism is only the other side of the same coin on which we have witnessed militant Islamism, the twin products of colonial modernity. No colonized nation has ever had an access to secularity (or self-concealing colonial Christianity as Gil Anidjar calls it) except through

DOI: 10.1057/9781137301291

the gun barrel of colonialism and thus colonial modernity. Secularism is colonialism in the guise of modernity. Agential autonomy, if the subaltern is to speak and not to be misunderstood, and its concomitant transition to democracy will have to be beyond the colonial condition in which we have come to know ourselves. That colonial condition is now transmuted into a neo-liberal/neo-conservative condition, and the restoration of agency will have to be in a post-Western critical imagination. To put it even more bluntly, secularism is not just Christianity in disguise or colonialism over-extended. Secularism *is* colonialism. Restoration of the polyvocal cosmopolitanism we have crafted and lived over the last two hundred years is the counter-culture that navigates beyond the colonial constitution of the secular or the religious that it ipso facto and paradoxically posits and legitimizes.

The worldliness I suggest here plays on an innate symbolic interactionism. Look at Chahar Shanbeh Suri, Noruz, Sizdah Bedar, and so on—on these occasions Iranians are using their Iranian registers against the Islamic Republic. This does not mean we are Zoroastrian and not Islamic—it means we shift the weight of our cultural identities in the opposition direction from the government, the same way that religious symbols were used against the Pahlavis, which gave the religious intellectuals the delusion that Iran is "essentially" a religious society. So the whole secular/religious thing is false binary because it places misplaced concretes on a social dynamism, in one swing or another—failing to see the society as a living organism in dialectical opposition to power—which points to the limits of governmentality, which makes even of Foucault a structural functionalist theorist of power. Chahar Shanbeh Suri tells you that people have a polyvocal register in their symbolic interactionism, an innate heteroglossia, always playing on a contrapuntal semiosis: "Charlie what are you rebelling against?"—What you got?

On veiling women, stoning the adulterers, or calling gays sick

How does this worldliness of the world—inserted between din and dowlat, register itself in the factual furies of our world, the world in which we live?

During the summer of 2012, as on Facebook and other social networking sites, young Iranian women were coming out of their mandatory veiling and giving public testimonials of their travail while forced to veil in

DOI: 10.1057/9781137301291

Iran, in a series of highly learned essays, Mohsen Kadivar went through excruciating details demonstrating how, according to his interpretation of the Qur'an and the Hadith and their commentaries in Sunni and Shi'i sources, Muslim women had to cover their bodies at least "from neck to knee," and expose nothing "except for the palms of their hands sand the oval of their face." "Covering the breasts is particularly important" he pinpointed. The importance of neck-to-knee coverage, he asserted, is entirely based in the Qur'an and not subject to time or location.[12]As Mohsen Kadivar was writing these essays, Massih Alinezhad, a prominent journalist who had recently opted to come out of the Islamic Republic's mandated veiling, continued to collect testimonies from scores of young Iranian women on her Facebook page, giving details of their fright and the humiliations they experienced while forcefully veiled in Iran.

Mohsen Kadivar is known, and rightly so, to be a fair and open-minded, even a progressive, cleric. He is on record for opposing mandatory veiling. He also believes in a secular democracy for his homeland. And yet in fulfilling his juridical duties as a high- ranking cleric he went through these canonical sources and was punctilious in explaining why it was necessary for Muslim women to cover their bodies according to the specifications he had extracted there from. His asserted his opinion from behind the habitual formality of his clerical robe, using the technical diction and declamation of a high-ranking cleric. Kadivar has attained the highest juridical education at Qom seminaries and studied Shi'i jurisprudence directly under the eminent Shi'i oppositional figure the late Ayatollah Montazeri. He now lives in exile. He is one of the most prominent oppositional figures identified with the Green Movement in Iran. He is the founding figure of *Jaras*, the leading oppositional website, which is deliberately and heroically standing up against the tyranny of the Islamic Republic. Still, his conception that Muslim women's bodies had to be covered had remained categorically limited to what he could competently make out as to the meaning and significance of the relevant Qur'anic and Hadith evidence.

Entirely irrelevant to Mohsen Kadivar, as is evident in this series of articles, is the basic question as to what these young women who were now escaping mandatory veiling and their homeland alike and voluntarily opting not to wear the veiling that the Islamic Republic and Mohsen Kadivar approved, were to do. Were they now considered excommunicated, no longer Muslims? And if so by what authority? Kadivar's authority, or the authority of the Islamic Republic that he opposed but

DOI: 10.1057/9781137301291

in this case effectively reproduced? And exactly who gave Kadivar or the Islamic Republic or the clerical establishment in Qom or Najaf that authority? If Muslim women dressed to show something of their body above their knee and below their neck or something of their breast, or something beyond the palm of their hands or the oval of their face, would they burn in hell, live and die in eternal shame and damnation? What would happen to their notions of piety, sanctity, or transcendence, to the God they knew and embraced, to the Prophet and the Imams that were dear to them, when they stopped following Kadivar's dress code? Myriad questions were raised when a leading oppositional cleric wrote so meticulously about how Muslim women were to dress—or else! Or else what, exactly?

Of course these women, born and bred as Muslims, were and remained Muslims as long as they so wished, in terms immediate and holy to their inner sanctity, and neither Kadivar nor the entire apparatus of the Islamic Republic nor the whole Islamic masculinist juridical apparatus combined had the power or the authority to tell them they were no longer Muslims just because they had decided not to accept Kadivar's deeply and irreversibly patriarchal mandate. The juridical disposition and discourse of both the Islamic Republic and the clerical class that Kadivar here represented was built to give these women a sense of shame, guilt, of having prostituted themselves to a frightful figment of these men's imagination they called *kofr* (blasphemy) or "the West." What astonishing hubris to assume that power and authority to terrorize people like that! Where were these women to abode after that metric disposition of their bodies, where were they to call home? What maddening sense of self-privilege would give a man or a group of men calling themselves *Rohaniyun* (the Spirituals) the power to write such things—and by what authority? The Qur'an and the Hadith were not their paternal inheritance. They belonged to the masses, to millions of Muslims to read or not read as they pleased, to place on their shelves reverentially and occasionally glance at, or even kiss, respectfully, or not. This was and remained their business. Of course these women were Muslims, by birth, by breeding, by culture, and by whatever force or factor of piety and faith that were sacrosanct to their own inner and innate sanctity as a Muslim, as a human being, and as a woman, a Muslim woman.

Kadivar, representing an entire history of falsely privileged juridicalism in Islam in general and in Shi'ism in particular, and thus categorically limited by their narrow reading of the sacred texts, is blinded to

DOI: 10.1057/9781137301291

the world he has inhabited, teaching as a guest professor on a North American university campus, where every day he would wake up and report to work, surrounded by women faculty and students who looked more like those Iranian Muslim women who had thrown away their veils than like the women he had envisioned popping out of those texts he had consulted in his library. Muslim women from one end of the Muslim world to another, from one end of the world to another, part of the work force, of the human habitat, looked and dressed in myriad forms. Kadivar was full of insights into those sources he was tabulating and yet entirely blinded to what he saw every day—the world he inhabited, the world that millions of Muslims—veiling or unveiling—had to call home.

Kadivar's sister, Jamileh Kadivar, an equally learned scholar of Shi'i scholasticism, had a couple of years earlier written an equally learned essay on stoning women and men to death on charges of adultery, generously concluding that because the barbaric act (my designation, not hers) was giving Islam a bad name, it had to be traded for other kinds of punishments. But only the hidden Infallible Imam was in a position to pass that particular judgment, and until he reappeared, no one was in a position to throw stones at people to kill them—and in the meantime alternative punishments were preferable to prevent *vahn-e Islam* (denigration of Islam).[13]This reasoning, of course, escaped other learned jurists, who evidently had a different reading of the selfsame sacred sources and continued ordering people stoned to death regularly. Jamileh Kadivar quotes a prominent cleric who had once told the late Ayatollah Khomeini, the founder of the Islamic Republic whom she refers to as "the Imam," about a conference in Europe on stoning in Islam. This cleric asked for Khomeini's permission to administer alternative punishments for adultery to prevent negative publicity against Islam. Khomeini agreed, and that became the rule of the land, despite the fact that in his own famous juridical tract, *Tahrir al-Wasilah*, Khomeini had approved of stoning. What sort of reasoning is that? Which of Khomeini's orders were people to follow—the command in his own *Tahrir al-Wasilah* or the verbal report of a prominent Ayatollah saying otherwise, and that not as a matter of principle, or even of logical reasoning, but just to prevent negative publicity against Islam? People continued to be stoned to death in Iran, even after that putative verbal report from Khomeini. Now what?

The problems with Jamileh Kadivar's myopic juridicalism are countless, among them, which learned Shi'i authority were we to believe and follow, and at what particular moment of their careers or even the time

DOI: 10.1057/9781137301291

of the day—the cleric in power who ordered people stoned to death on proof or even on the assumption of adultery, or the one not in power but still going meticulously through her sources to argue that no one had the authority to pass that judgment except the Hidden Imam, or the cleric-king in power who wanted to wage a publicity campaign to prevent the denigration of Islam? Even more seriously, if we are to believe Jamileh Kadivar's line of argument, what is the obvious implication of the assertion that only the Hidden Infallible Imam could stone people to death—that we as believing Shi'is would be left wondering whether we should continue to wish for the reappearance of the Hidden Imam, knowing that he will appear, throwing stones first at people who were charged with adultery? Was that the image we are to have of our Hidden Imam—exactly at the moment that he is coming back to establish eternal justice in the world?

Fortunately, exacting and onerous juridical clerics like Jamileh Kadivar and Mohsen Kadivar have always been in minority in Islamic societies and intellectual history. Their fixation on legalism has scarcely gone unchallenged by philosophers, mystics, poets, and the literati. The fact of Islamic law has always been located in the polyvocal phenomenon of the Islamic intellectual disposition. It is only by an accident of history that for the last 200 years the clerical class in Iran has coagulated into a fraternity, whose members are convinced that they have an exclusive claim on interpreting Islam for Muslims at large. They don't. No one ever gave them that authority. They gave themselves that power and from a sustained attitude of self-referentiality claimed that power. We as Muslims are free to read or even not to read, interpret or introvert, manifest or hold private to our own mind and soul our sacred texts in any which way we want, any which way we damn or bless please. There are as many ways to God as there are human beings, as there are Muslims, and nobody died and made Kadivar or his sister or the self-asserting clerical juridicalism they represent the arbiter of truth in all matters Islamic. They categorically reduce our humanity to a fictive juridical subject over which they then claim absolutist authority. But we are not juridical tropes, we are humans, we have the God given right of fallibility, the gift of reason, the freedom of choice, of heteroglossia, of polyfocality.

A Muslim woman can wear whatever she pleases and still be a Muslim. Thousands upon thousands of Muslim women are victims of global trafficking, forced into prostitution by a cruel fate—and all Kadivar's *Islam-e Rahmani* can offer them is a measuring tape to cover themselves from

DOI: 10.1057/9781137301291

neck to knee, with the stipulation that "breasts are particularly important?" Are those Muslim women not women, not Muslim? The insanity of this fixation with juridicalism boggles the mind. A man or a woman who commits adultery should not be stoned to death. He or she should just deal with the worldly, heartbreaking or liberating, consequences of their actions within the privacy of the bond of love or a marriage that had once held them together. No honor killing, so-called, no stoning to death—just parting ways and finding happiness somewhere else. That's all—and doing so without the falsely assumed power of excommunicating anyone from being a Muslim. An adulterous Muslim is still a Muslim, a Muslim prostitute is still a Muslim, entitled to her or his life and liberty. We don't start with our texts and go to the world to cut and paste it to our liking. We start with the world and go back to our texts to find a moral and forgiving frame of reference for that world. We start with a Muslim teenager from anywhere in the world sold into sexual slavery, we find a passage in the canonical texts that offers haven and solace to those frightened bones. We do not pick up a measuring tape and become a juridical tailor to those remnants of broken humanity. What sort of a jurist would abandon the spirit of justice for the letter of the law?

This is the supreme calamity of the Islamic Republic that has so categorically ingrained its power that even those who actively oppose it think they are in charge of defining our faith for us, or being the gatekeepers to our being a Muslim in this world. They are not. A few years ago in London, I was driving with a prominent reformist activist who was close to Khatami and Mousavi, a young doctoral student whom I dearly like and admire. During our casual conversation, I said something in which he picked up the phrase "I as a Muslim." He looked at me with bright eyes and asked, "So you consider yourself a Muslim?" "Of course I do," I said, "what sort of a question is that?" "We very much welcome that," he said with an endearing smile. "We," I asked pointedly, "who are "we?" He pulled back in wonder. "Who are you or your entire coterie of the so-called 'religious intellectuals' to admit me into my own faith. I, a *bechcheh Shi'a* (I deliberately used a colloquial Persian phrase, literally, 'I, a Shi'i child') born to a devout Shi'i mother, in Ahvaz, a whole clime and culture away from your capital city and your 'religious intellectuals?'" I had a faint smile on my face to soften the blow, so I could pull him back to listen. He did.

The late Ali Shari'ati spent a lifetime trying to pull Islam (Shi'ism in particular) into the public domain and away from its self-appointed

DOI: 10.1057/9781137301291

juridical custodians—only to be brushed aside by Khomeini and his clerical clique who were claiming a world and worldly religion back for their own class. In the case of Kadivar, his textual juridicalism remains entirely oblivious to the moral and political forces of our post-modern condition—and thus to the nightmare of the juridical absolutism that life itself is subject of exacting juridical tyranny. Kadivar seems to be entirely oblivious to the fact that the body he wants to subject to exacting juridical measurements and concealment is already stripped naked and exposed—far beyond his scholastic sources and vocabulary—by a judicial machinery that rules over his power and authority. He is too fixated on his juridical sources even to notice that power, even while teaching at a North American university campus. His eyes are so scholastically fixated that he does not see the body that he wishes to cover from the naked eyes is already politically stripped beyond any juridical concealment. Because of that blindness, Kadivar's scholasticism doubly indemnifies the body and the body politics of Muslims in their post-modern predicament, subjugated to a frightful juridical machinery that seeks to conceal the female body with the same scholastic exactitude with which that very same body is juridically regulated and tortured in the same Islamic republic he thinks opposes but in fact corroborates and reiterates. Those torturers practice with whips and lashes what Kadivar theorizes for them with his jurisprudence—the physical and verbal discipline of the body via an aggressive reduction of our *carpus humanitas* to *a juridical body*. Although on their limited political field they may think they oppose each other, the jurist and the torturer are in effect corroborating each other and further exacerbating the aggressive and violent transmutation of our bodies into sites of juridical psychosis.

The foundational fear of losing control over body politics has projected itself into a juridical will to control, regulate, and legislate the human body. The constitution of the Islamic Republic, over which presides the absolutist power of the Supreme Jurist (ValiFaqih)—Kadivar's prototype even when he opposes him—is a mere territorial reflection of the Shi'i jurist's habitual penchant to legislate the human body. The fear of losing control over the body of the Muslim believer—a woman who is not juridically clothed, a gay who is not juridically sexed, an adulterer who is not juridically desirous—is deeply rooted in an elitist assumption of control over the Muslim body politics. Though the issue might be extended to Islamic law in general, it has a peculiar Shi'i dimension to it.

DOI: 10.1057/9781137301291

A key factor here is the constitutionally undemocratic disposition of the clerical establishment (the so-called *Rohaniyun* institution). Predicated on the charismatic memory of the Shi'i Imams, this institution harbors a deeply presumptuous assumption about its authority over the Muslim community—in the absence of the Hidden Imam, acting as if they act on his behalf. A deeply rooted (but misplaced) arrogance informs this clerical class—long since overdue to be reminded that their entire curricular program in what passes for scholastic learning in Qom or Najaf these days will not amount to even a proper MA degree in a respectable university anywhere else in the world. Predicated on that false assurance, the clerical class assumes an air of authority over the masses of Muslim believers that in reality it lacks. All it takes is a Facebook page these days to have a solid record of ordinary Muslims defying this clerical class—but if Facebook is not an accurate barometer of the society at large, neither is the seminarian milieu of these clerics in Qom or Najaf. Fortunately, the overwhelming majority of Muslims who are Sunni do not suffer from such impediments—for among them there is no clerical class of the sort that rules Qom and has now by extension been ruling Iran and has even procreated itself among the clerical opposition.

The juridical exactitude with which the Shi'i cleric wishes to control the body is particularly anxiety ridden when confronted with the homoerotic body. A young Muslim man writes to Kadivar and begins his letter by saying, "man pesar Mosalmani hastam keh beh hamjens gara'i tamayol daram (I am a Muslim boy who is inclined towards homosexuality) and then asks his opinion about permission to marry another homosexual man. Kadivar picks up an innocent phrase from the young man's question and categorically identifies homosexuality as "genetic confusion," and thus as an illness that needs to be properly diagnosed and medically treated.[14]The gendered body is the space *par excellence* of the juridical discourse of power. Men are men, women are women, and anyone who thinks or acts or feels otherwise than thus mandated in the juridically gendered sexuality ought to be a degenerate oddity. Clerical jurists like Kadivar have of course every right to opine on any matter they wish, but only as citizens of a healthy society and a free and democratic republic where other Muslims or non-Muslims have identical rights to help form and shift the public opinion—and certainly not at a time when their clerical cohorts are using and abusing the selfsame jurisprudence ruthlessly to rule over the life and liberty of people who may not share their opinions.

DOI: 10.1057/9781137301291

Muslims in their worlds

The separation of din and dowlat is no longer sufficient without the intermediary of donya that must intervene to open up the space in which the clerical class and their scholastic juridicalism is blindly trapped. It will make no difference if the Islamic Republic and Ayatollah Khamenei go and a secular democracy and Ayatollah Kadivar go back. It will be the same. He will still take a tape measure and decide from where on the neck to where on the knee women's bodies must be covered, and to what clinic gays and lesbians must report to get cured. He and his fraternity club are constitutionally blinded to the fact that the body they keep measuring is always already naked and that nakedness can only be covered by civil liberties—their *zoë* becoming *bios* for a sane and civil living, which means the thick and thickening rope of "the Islamic" must be taken away from the thin neck of "the republic" not just in name but in mentality, in the governmentality that is definitive to the Islamic law, which is so juridically fixated on the body that demands absolutist control of the body politics. Islam must be entrusted to Muslims, and Muslims to their worlds.

To come to terms with the world in which Muslims live requires a radical reconsideration of the relation between this and the other world—the sacred sanctity that governs Muslims' worldliness. On what terms din and dowlat can be separated—what it means to ask for a secular politics, divorced from people's sacred certitudes—is entirely contingent on coming to terms with the fact and the phenomenon of the world and worldliness. Din, dowlat, and donya must come together to raise the linguistic horizon we need to come ashore to a new globality of our consciousness. We need to rethink these concepts for, as Gadamer noted, "a view of the language is a view of the world"—and it is precisely that language that needs to be altered to be in tune with the world that is emerging. In that language, the forced binary between a tyrannical theocracy and a militant secularism is a false choice, without taking full account of the world a Muslim must come to terms with in order to cultivate a new sense and intuition of the sacred.

With an urgency far more critical than that with which Habermas gathered German intellectuals in 1979, Ahmad Sadri had in 2010 invited their Iranian counterparts to Lake Forest to wonder "the spiritual situation of our age," which is the political crisis of not just the Islamic Republic, but the moral crisis of Islam itself, "the Islam" that was posited against

DOI: 10.1057/9781137301291

"the West." With "the West" having imploded, Islam now does not yet know to whom it is talking—and that is a good thing for Muslims can now learn a language with which they can bypass their self-appointed clerical custodians. Toward the articulation of the grammatology of that language, the polyvocality of Islam must be released from the domain of the din and the binary of din and dowlat, and allowed to be returned to the world Muslims now inhabit, like a fish back to the sea, with no undue anxiety, for as Hujwiri says in *Kashf al-Mahjub*, "when there was Sufism there was no name for it and when there was a name for it there was no Sufism." Replace Islam for Sufism, see "the West" implode somewhere over the Atlantic in the post-9/11 map of the world, let din and dowlat absolve into donya, and let us all celebrate the birth of the first Muslim citizen.

Notes

1   See Jürgen Habermas (ed.), *Observations on "The Spiritual Situation of the Age"* (Cambridge, MA: MIT Press, 1979/1984).

2   Ibid: viii.

3   For more details on these kangaroo courts see Hamid Dabashi, "A Tale of Two Cities" (*al-Ahram Weekly*, August 20–26, 2009). Available online at http://weekly.ahram.org.eg/2009/961/op51.htm

4   See Mohammad Reza Nikfar, "Elahiyat-e Shekanjah/Theology of Torture" (*Nilgoon*: 10 Shahrivar 1388/September 1, 2009). Available at http://www.nilgoon.org/archive/mohammadrezanikfar/articles/Nikfar_Theology_of_Torture.html

5   For further exchanges between Nikfar and Kadivar see: http://kadivar.com/?p=6134. For my contribution to the debate see http://www.rahesabz.net/story/14504/. For a critical assessment of these debates see http://zamaaneh.com/idea/2010/06/post_736.html#fn3. For a complete list of all those engaged in the debate see http://www.facebook.com/note.php?note_id=297279336981865. All these debates are in Persian, and they continue by other commentators apace.

6   See Francis Fukuyama, *The End of History and the Last Man* (New York: Harper Perennial 1993).

7   See Edward Said, "Traveling Theory," a critique of Michel Foucault conception of power, in *The World, the Text, and the Critic* (Cambridge, MA: Harvard University Press, 1983): 243–247.

8   See Giorgio Agamben, *Homo Sacer: Sovereign Power and Bare Life*. Translated by Daniel Heller-Roazen (Palo Alto, CA: Stanford University Press, 1998),

DOI: 10.1057/9781137301291

and Giorgio Agamben, *Remnants of Auschwitz: The Witness and the Archive*. Translated by Daniel Heller-Roazen (New York: Zone, Books, 2002).

9   Agamben, *Remnants of Auschwitz*: 41–43.

10 For further details see Andrew Buchwalter's introduction to his translation of Habermas's *Observations on "The Spiritual Situation of the Age"* (op. cit.): xv.

11 For details of this undaunted vulgarity see this report (in Persian): http://www.radiofarda.com/content/F11_Iran_postelection_Daneshju_university/2140659.html

12 See Mohsen Kadivar, "Ta'mmolidar Mas'aleh-ye Hejab/Reflection on the Question of Hijab" (*Jaras*, July 29, 2012). Available at http://www.rahesabz.net/story/56968/. Accessed August 23, 2012. See also "Hejabdar Ravayatva Fatawi Ahl-e Sonnat/Veiling in the Narratives and Fatwas of the Sunnis" (*Jaras*, August 16, 2012).Available at http://www.rahesabz.net/story/57654/. Accessed August 23, 2012.

13 See "Sangsar, Islam, va Doran-e Mo'aser/Stoning, Islam, and the Contemporary Times" *(MajallehFeministi*, August 15, 2010). Available at http://www.feministschool.com/spip.php?article5472. Accessed August 25, 2012.

14 See "Adam Javaz Rabeteh Jensiva Ezdevajba Hamjens/The Impermissibility of Sexual Relations and Marriage of the Same Sex" (official website of Mohsen Kadivar, June–July 2012). Available at http://kadivar.com/?p=9491. Accessed August 26, 2012.

DOI: 10.1057/9781137301291

6

"Religion—Quote, Unquote"

Abstract: *In Chapter 6, I turn to the term "religion," to wonder in what way we may come to terms with what it entails and all the alterities it implicates. The world exists as a world because of the worldly disposition of the language that facilitates the reading of that world as a lived experience. "Not only is the world 'world' only insofar as it comes into language, but language, too, has its real being only in the fact that the world is re-presented within it." That Gadamerian insight will guide our way toward a renewed conception of "religion."*

Dabashi, Hamid. *Being a Muslim in the World.*
New York: Palgrave Macmillan, 2013. DOI:
10.1057/9781137301291.

Let me begin where I left off in the last chapter, with two citations from the ends of a wide historical spectrum:

> When there was Sufism there was no name for it, when there was a name for it, there was no Sufism.
>
> —Abu al-Hasan al-Hujwiri, Kashf al-Mahjub, eleventh century

And Christianity turned against itself in a complex and ambivalent series of parallel movements...while slowly coming to name that to which it ultimately claimed to oppose itself: religion. Munchausen-like, it attempted to liberate itself, to extricate itself from its own conditions; it judged itself no longer Christian, no longer religious. Christianity (that is, to clarify this one last time, Western Christendom) judged and named itself, it reincarnated itself as secular.

> —Gil Anidjar, "Secularism," 2006

Imagine a canopy in the middle of an unnamed desert, for naming is everything, or smack in the middle of New York City's Times Square, in the un-time of our own history and habitat! Upon that canopy is written a strange aphorism: When there was Sufism there was no name for it, when there was a name for it, there was no Sufism. How are we to read that which I have the choice of not naming a paradox? I dwell under and invite you into the shade of that canopy, to paraphrase Abu al-Hasan al-Hujwiri's eleventh century (that would be on Christian, not al-Hujwiri's own time) phrase and suggest: When there was Religion there was no name for it, when there was a name for it, there was no Religion.

Addressing the changing ways that religion, thus named, "impinges on scholarship" in a wide range of fields (for that is our task)—from literature and history to philosophy, law, biology, sociology, anthropology, and above all, the discipline that calls itself religious studies, or just religion, and thus, religion Itself—must begin with the origin and the end, nature and disposition, of this very impinging. Why, whence, wherefore, and by what authority, this impinging—this colliding, encroaching, and above all, trespassing? In what he called "the sacred order," my late teacher Philip Rieff in fact took this impinging, which he named "transgression," as the defining moment when the No, the Thou Shalt Not, or what he called the "interdiction," that made, and unmade, what we have the choice of not calling religion possible—though for him the Sacred Order was the art and the jurisprudence of the impossible.

DOI: 10.1057/9781137301291

He did, in his Sacred Order, stipulate certain remissive occasions, of course, and they acted as merciful bumper zones between the veracity of the interdictions and the ferocity with which transgressions assailed them, which stipulation made his vision of the highest order, sustaining civility via the civilizing function of Freudian repression (which he thought tantamount to "revelation"), historically anchored and worldly wise. It is precisely that historical anchorage and that worldly wisdom I wish to retrieve by way of releasing scholarship from the self-imposed pre-occupation with, the burden of, I might even say, this thing I have a choice not to call religion.[1]

The christening of religion

I thus begin not with al-Hujwiri, in whose comfortable shadow I sit, or with Rieff, with whom I learned how to think about religion, with and without quotation marks, where he as a Jewish master and I as a Muslim disciple convened, or with Freud whose repression Rieff taught me read as revelation, but with Gil Anidjar—friend, colleague, comrade, the precocious rabbi in casual disguise. I will begin where Gil Anidjar recently ended, for he ended where we should have started—by saying that religion is the invention of Christianity, so that it (Christianity, Western Christianity, he insists) can hide itself under the guise of secularism, that secularism is Christianity and religion its doppelgänger. Under the shade and shadow of al-Hujwiri I wish to go upstream from Gil Anidjar and wonder what was Christianity thinking, if that is what Christianity was doing and if I were to stay the course with Gil Anidjar, when it invented religion to distance and hide itself under secularism?[2]

Going upstream, the question remains the same: Who in the world invented this thing that scholars, comedians, politicians, and terrorists call "religion—quote unquote." Rather than thinking secularism the invention of Christianity (or even Western Christianity, as Gil Anidjar keeps stipulating and assuring himself and others), I wish to exonerate Christianity from any such involvement and to call attention to the history I have the choice of naming *the colonial condition of Christianity* as the culprit. In other words, I wish to unpack the moment of anxiety when Gil Anidjar keeps correcting himself that "Western Christianity," not Christianity as such, is the culprit. The adjectival "Western" does not clarify the condition in which Christianity is believed to have invented

DOI: 10.1057/9781137301291

religion but hides it—a Freudian hiding that betrays the hiding place. Instead of diagnosing "Western Christianity," a double negative, with Munchausen syndrome in absentia, I sit under the shade of this canopy, where I have invited you to join me, and wonder if Christianity itself is not equally at the receiving end of the colonial invention of religion, a colonialism that Christianity may have well served since Juan Ginés de Sepúlveda (1489–1573), but has equally confronted ever since his nemesis and contemporary Bartolomé de las Casas. In our own terms, I am not ready to relinquish Christianity to Cardinal Ratzinger, a.k.a His Holiness Pope Pious XVI, but allow Father Gustavo Gutiérrez to have a say in the matter—and when and if I do that, the sea that separates the Holy Sea from the liberation theologian is not the chimerical curiosity called "the West" but the traumatic experience code-named colonialism.

In his seminal work, *Genealogies of Religion* (1993), Talal Asad questioned the universal validity of the notion and the trope of "religion" and excavated its conceptual roots as a historical category in European modernity.[3] He contended that the twin towers of secularism and religion were in fact conceptually coterminous—one liberal and liberating, and the other repressive and thus relegated to the private sphere (from the public sphere) throughout the course of European modernity, which I insist on calling "colonial modernity." Asad's argument ultimately put forward the proposition that the category of "religion" was the invention of this European colonial modernity, an invention that has ipso facto enabled a particular mode of historicity, historiography, and history making. The category "religion" was thus an enabling force—it invented and enabled "the West," and its corollaries (liberal democracy, Western secularism, and above all, capitalist modernity), and there, right there, is the rub. For this very capitalist modernity has its own twin tower of colonialism that has yet to be grasped as a transformative force and power, not just on the peripheralized reaches of the world, but in its self-appointed centers. Capitalism *is* colonialism—and capitalist modernity *is* colonial modernity—and that modernity has had a catalytic impact on just about everything it touched, from the heavens to the earth.

The colonial condition of the capital christening of religion

Talal Asad's idea of religion as a manufactured anthropological category already points to the colonial disposition of the ethnographic project

DOI: 10.1057/9781137301291

in contradistinction to that of sociology. Sociology was something that sociologists did *here* (the metaphysical *here*) while anthropology was something that anthropologists did *there* (the metaphysical *there*).The disciplinary binary between sociological method and anthropological ethnography ipso facto points to the enabling binary of "the West and the Rest," that "the West" was where the capital *Geselleschaft* had happened, and "the Rest" where the colonial *Gemeinschaft* was the *condito sine qua non* of being-in-the world—which proposition in the specific case of "Islam and the West" has been particularly troublesome in the course of colonial modernity.[4]

My contention is that to come to terms with the invention of religion, we need to explore the colonial disposition of the modernity that crafted it in the first place. For I take the European adventure of modernity not just to have an extended colonial shadow, but in fact to be colonial in its origin and disposition, character and culture. Talal Asad was conscious of this colonial disposition when he warned that "hasty readers might conclude that my discussion of the Christian religion is skewed toward an authoritarian, centralized, elite perspective, and that consequently it fails to take into account the religions of the heterodox believers, of resistant peasantries, of all those who cannot be completely controlled by the Orthodox church."[5]That specific stipulation, however, needs to pan out to a wider range of theoretical implications.

If we were to allow the rude intrusion of the colonial nuisance into the matter, then the two critical forces—historicity and worldliness—have something to say about when and how the naming and the nomos of religion (as the Unreason of the Reason that was to cause and condition colonial modernity) came about, and how we may in fact save it from its own name, un-name it, de-name it, return it to the sea it came from, where it can breathe and swim, unbeknownst to itself, as it must. For that self-knowledge has become self-conscious, and has amounted to violently awkward behavior.

If we allow the nuisance and the impolite act of colonialism to announce itself, we will see that the invention of religion was an historical act of alienation, of fetishization, of commodification, of the depletion of the world of and in itself, the capital crafting of a vacuity that would make the world into merchandise, marketable to itself. "Religion" was invented in, by, for, and in the course of capitalist modernity. The Protestant ethic may have conditioned the rise of capitalism, as Max Weber suggested, but capitalism more than returned the favor when it

DOI: 10.1057/9781137301291

invented Protestantism as a religion, and with it a sociology of religion to which Max Weber became a Socratic midwife, delivering and bringing religion into this world—for when there was religion there was no sociology (or anthropology or a Muslim terrorist or a Jewish settler or a Christian Zionist or a standup comedian) for it, and when there was a sociology for it there was no religion.

But sociology (like all other disciplinary inventions of modernity) was itself one of many modus operandi of capitalist modernity, so that the invention of religion was geared to alienate the world from itself, project that alienation inward and outward, and fight the ghost of its own invention in the name of secularity. The self-circuitous circularity of this secularity then began to hide its own casuistry by attacking the ghost of its own invention that it now called "religion."

It was the material force of the ipso facto (and always already) globalized capital, and the colonial modernity it enabled as its most potent universalizing machinery, and not the vacuous propensities of Christianity, which as much enforced as resisted capitalism, that invented religion in the colonial corners of its operation in order to call itself secular at the presumed center of its globality. The insistence of Gil Anidjar (in effect repeating Talal Asad's) that interrupts him every time he says Christianity and adds parenthetically that it is "Western Christianity" he has in mind, is precisely because he knows but does not make the leap to the fact that Christianity posits a vacuity that has no agency. Capital does—particularly on its colonial site and citations. By "colonial" I have nothing fancy in mind. Colonial to me is the vertical abuse of labor by capital run horizontally amuck all over the globe. Capital called itself "secular" (or, alternatively, "modern") at the European center of its manufactured globality and then denied, denigrated, dismissed, and sought to subjugate all its colonial sites to religion (or, alternatively, "tradition") in order to belittle, intimidate, dismiss, and dominate them. Capital had the same disdain for the colonial site, which it called "religion," as for its own feudal European past, which it held (as it invented and catapulted it onto its medieval and ancient shores) even in darker contempt.

Commodity fetishization of religion and its doppelgänger

Religion is not just the twin tower of secularism. It *is* secularism. There are no twin towers. There is only one—reflecting itself to itself. Religion

DOI: 10.1057/9781137301291

is secularism, as you can see if you look and listen to each one carefully. Secularism is not just the doppelganger of religion. It is it. The one has conspired with itself to look like two, like twins, like mirror images, the mirage of a mirage. In his "secularism," Gil Anidjar picked up where Talal Asad had left off and what Edward Said had hidden, and sought to show how Christianity, in his estimation, invented religion as a place where it could house its own symptomatic anxiety and thus run for cover and hide itself under secularism—by the same logic, I guess the best place to hide a stolen property is the police station. But I am not sure that singularity of intention of the text (Christianity), the author (the Church), or the readers (Christians)—if I use Umberto Eco's hermeneutics—can sustain itself. Secularity is not just Christianity. Secularity is also Islam, Judaism, Buddhism, Hinduism, Zoroastrianism, and Manichaeism fetishized. Secularism is the somber graveyard and the august pantheon of its own manufactured alterities, code-named religions, which in distinguishing, denying, attacking, or even befriending each other negate each other, and in so doing authenticate the self-conscious illegitimacy of the bourgeois banality that has designated itself as secular. Secularity is religion's greatest invention, and the other way around. Secularity is religion in the speculum of its own other, the other of its own making—that is why fundamentalists of all brands and fanatical secularists of all nations look and act and talk and behave so alike. Secularism and religion are one battle over two representations, over the mimetic might of one story over another.

Secularism and religion are like the two parts of Martin Scorsese's *Shutter Island* (2010).For half of the film US marshal Teddy Daniels (Leonardo DiCaprio) and his partner Chuck Aule (Mark Ruffalo) travel to the Ashecliff Hospital for the criminally insane on Shutter Island to investigate the disappearance of Rachel Solando (Emily Mortimer), a patient who has mysteriously vanished from a locked room. In the second half of the film, the selfsame Teddy Daniels becomes Andrew Laeddis, who had murdered his manic depressive wife after she had drowned their three children, and then created a fantasy in which he was a war hero to cope with his own trauma. So, which is which—is Teddy Daniels a US marshal investigating secret US government experiments that use psychotropic medication to master mind control and create sleeper agents for use in the Cold War? Or, is he Andrew Laeddis, a criminally insane inmate inventing delusions to cope with the pain of having murdered his own criminally insane wife? The film (contrary to

DOI: 10.1057/9781137301291

many critics' misreading of it) is entirely inconclusive. The playful master filmmaker Martin Scorsese uses it to flaunt the power of cinema to craft equally compelling delusions, and we leave the theater not so much baffled as to what has happened but befuddled by the sheer power of the magic we call cinema. Just like Teddy Daniels and Andrew Laeddis, religion and secularism are each other's mirror image, one and the same, each taking the other for an illusion, both pretending they are a reaction to the other—one has invented the other, and it no longer matters which is which, for we are at the mercy of both, dis-inventing each other.

Religion: the name for de-worlding the world

Colonial modernity's invention of religion robbed the world of its quiet certitude and gave it the gaudiness of a trademark, which was fetishized like all other commodities. The moment Marx, the first and final theorist of capital, said, "religion is…" religion was already invented. The moment when Marx said, "religion is the opium of the masses," he had excavated the false consciousness he needed to make the masses in want of an ideology he thought he was giving them, like drug addicts that are made as such and then told they are addicted and given a new sedative—ideology. The moment Marx said, "religion is the sigh of the oppressed creature, the heart of a heartless world, just as it is the spirit of a spiritless situation," he gave birth to and became the first witness to an oppressed creature that needed to scream "workers of the world unite," instead of sighing uselessly. Religion was the sigh Marx breathed, exhaling forcefully so that his oppressed creatures would scream even louder. "Heartless world" was the name of the moment when Marx himself depleted the world of its worldliness to fill it out with a heartfelt romanticism, a spiritless situation. The supreme theorist of the fetishized commodity at once commodified and fetishized the world and called it religion, thus, ipso facto, alienating the world from itself. Marx became the sign and the signifier and the paramount sample of his own insight. Marx was not a Marxist, as he himself put it.

"Tradition" was the greatest invention of European colonial modernity, and "religion" the most modern of all traditions. The invention of religion by modernity sought to authenticate the otherwise circuitous disposition of secularism by delegating a fictive pre-secularity to it in temporal and territorial terms—as it temporally catapulted it to the back

DOI: 10.1057/9781137301291

end of European history, it also at the same time pre-postponed it to the other (non-European) parts of the world. "The West" thus became secular by way of "the Rest" becoming religious. Religion is thus an invention of colonial modernity in conclusive defense of its globalizing enterprise. Secularity is European colonialism run metaphysically counterintuitive.

Nor was Europe (in its own varied histories and geographies) spared the conceptual cannibalization of its own making. Before it became the invention of the Third World, as Fanon aptly put it, Europe had started cannibalizing its own pre-modern history as ferociously as it had colonized the rest of the world. Religion did vertically to European history what it had done horizontally to global geography—designating and dismissing the medieval and Jerusalem as religion and constituting and claiming the Renaissance and Greece as secular. Secularism was not the invention of Christianity, as Gil Anidjar suggests; religion was the invention of colonial modernity as it depleted the world of not just its natural resources but also its *worldly* disposition, replenishing it with a divisive alienation from itself—tradition versus modernity, Islam versus the West, the West versus the Rest, the Sacred versus the Profane. It is not just the world that needs to be freed from Europe as a colonial state of mind; Europe needs to be rescued from Europe. The European post-coloniality, now in full swing, is what we call anything from post-modernity to post-structuralism, whereby Europe is ever so gently de-Europeanizing itself. The Eurozone economic crisis, the labor and student unrest from Greece to Spain, the rise of the Indignados are all coming together, not just to dissolve the very idea of Europe and its Euro, but also to link the continental uprising to the rest of the world via the Arab Spring. The rise of ethnic nationalism and the appearance of Christian supremacist mass murderers like Anders Breivik are the nervous signs of this eventuality.

The aggressive commodification and subsequent fetishization of the world—including but not limited to religion—depleted it of its varied modes of signifying and marking worldliness. Things became their signs, and signs were fixated in the vacuous semiotics of a self-hallowing tableau that meant nothing but marked everything. Adorno's "culture industry" saw and sold religion (which he called "theology") like any other brand, and the selfsame religion became definitive to *the society of spectacle* long before Guy Debord saw and theorized the event. As colonial modernity fixed and fetishized religion—as something menacing in the European public past now better privatized (in more than one sense), and as something still public, embarrassing, a nuisance on

DOI: 10.1057/9781137301291

the colonial site, religious movements became the vindictive return of a diligently repressed reality—the defiant sigh of the repressed for real. The Enlightenment pushing of religion into the *private* space ipso facto *privatized* religion much the same way the US military has now privatized its various chores (including torturing people). Xe Services LLC or Blackwater USA, and now its globalized version Blackwater Worldwide, are "religion"—or religion is to faith what Blackwater is to military—par excellence. Christian fundamentalism, militant Zionism, apocalyptic Islamism, combative Hinduism, and insurrectionary Buddhism—and their entire collective penchant for iconic violence—became the violent signs and signals of the return of the repressed, and thus a sign that religion had reached the point of moral and political meltdown. Osama bin Laden was now Islam, as Baruch Goldstein was Judaism; the Gujarat massacre of Muslims, Hinduism. Seung-Hui Cho's massacre at Virginia Tech, and Donald Rumsfeld's campaign of "shock and awe" in Iraq competed for Christianity. Religion in its fetishized form was devouring itself, waging violence solely for spectacular and iconic reasons. It is thus revealed that religion knows of its dubious, fetishized, and vacuous origins and covers itself by appealing to metaphysics of violence that hides behind spectacular violence its anxiogenic disposition.

Terrorists (Osama bin Laden and Babu Bajrangi), comedians (Bill Maher and Christopher Hitchens), politicians (George W. Bush and Mahmoud Ahmadinejad), and professors of religion (our own gathering in Lake Forest) are all implicit in the acts of religion. To study religion is to indulge in the convoluted metaphysics of transparency in which religion is now packaged, staged, and sold. Departments and disciplines of religious studies are paradigmatic of a false (commodified) consciousness turned against itself. I recall how, as a graduate student and junior faculty, the number of words assigned to me by editors of leading scholarly journals in our fields to review a book or write an essay on modern Islam increased proportionately to any hijacking or kidnapping by the Shi'i militia in Lebanon. Studying an epiphenomenon that keeps alienating the world in and of itself has made academic careers contingent on a false premise that keeps authenticating itself.

Un-naming religion, re-worlding the world

Dis-inventing religion does not commence, cannot begin, with shaming Christianity, or even (exacerbating the misplaced concreteness)

DOI: 10.1057/9781137301291

with Western Christianity. The hidden anxiety of colonial modernity embedded in the dying signifier "Western" needs a far more careful and perhaps even urgent autopsy. Reclaiming that which I have the choice of not naming "faith" begins with re-worlding the world, retrieving the polyvocal heteronormativity that capital had to treat like any other raw material, crush, quell, commodify, and pacify in order to make world safe for commodity, colonialism, secularism, Halliburton, Blackwater Worldwide, and (of course, by all means) democracy and human rights. Dis-inventing religion and all its ruses (from militant secularism to colonial modernity) commences with re-worlding the world by imagining the multiple universes, varied worlds, that it has historically denied, denigrated, and overcome—or more accurately, treated as raw material and commodified. Recall that in the three Kantian moments of the first through the third critique, we (the colonial folks), were never part of the knowing subject, but part of the knowable world, and that is why the European author of "Was istAufklärung?" (1784) considered our sort of art "grotesque" and us incapable of the sublime and the beautiful.

Re-worlding the world means forgetting about religion, and allowing it (cross that pronoun) yet again not to have a name—to un-name the named, and let it be, where it matters, like the invisible air you breathe, and that you notice only when you lack it. To dis-invent religion and re-world the world, let me take advantage of my Manichean mannerism and summon the three wise Magi who never made it to Bethlehem, to bear witness to the world before and after religion, where you can see how the world has been busily at work re-worlding itself, in literature and cinema, poetry and politics—where the face of the other has become the site and citation of not just an alterity, but an alterity coming home to be at ease with its self.

Let me then use my privileged position and invoke my Manichean mannerism to summon those three wise Magi and wonder how the world can be re-worlded. Behold the three wise Magi: Aquinas, Al-Ghazali, and Maimonides. Before they were dubbed "religious philosophers" they had no clue that this is what they were. Place their seminal texts in front of you—*al-Munqidh min al-Dalal (Deliverance from Error)*, *Summa Theologica*, and *Moreh Nevuchim/ Dalalat al-Ha'irin (The Guide for the Perplexed)*. They have been talking to each other in Arabic, Latin, and Hebrew as fellow students of one distant Greek sage, overcoming their teacher in their own ways. Before "the West" was invented and these three Aristotelians were sent to opposing sides of "Islam and the West,"

DOI: 10.1057/9781137301291

philosophy had a different history, religion was nowhere in sight, and the Mediterranean basin was the locus classicus of, not just seafarers and fairytales, but also a manner of worldliness yet to be retrieved, re-imagined.

Now meet the three wise Magi: Nietzsche, Kierkegaard, and Dostoyevsky. None took philosophy seriously, or knew where philosophy ended and literature began, or, a fortiori, when fear and trembling as acts of faith were allowed to be called religion. They did not trespass or cross any border they could not see. The border of religion crossed them. But by standing still, right where they were, unable to do otherwise, they defied the semantic sovereignty of that which calls itself religion. Now meet the three wise Magi: Marx, Weber, and Durkheim, who invented religion as the alterity of Reason, as the opium of the masses and alienation, as the Protestant ethics that inadvertently spirited capitalism, or as the modus operandi of a conscious collective that had to be placed among the Australian aborigines in order to make sense of the layered subconscious of European societies.

Now meet the three wise Magi: Freud, Jung, and Kafka, where the outline of a collective subconscious mapped out the realm of repression to summon the modernity of man in front of the Law, or else in a penal colony. Now meet the three wise Magi: Philip Rieff, Martin Buber, and Reinhold Niebuhr—to tease out and unleash the sense of the scared from religion, posit an existential face to face between I-and-Thou for it, or bring Marxism to bear on American Christianity. Now meet the three wise Magi: Foucault, Levinas, and Derrida, where they meet to confirm religion in an Islamic Revolution but fail to see it in the face of the Palestinian other, or as a radical negative theology, or a Nietzschean free play of signifiers that seeks to free religion from religion.

Now meet the three wise Magi: Peruvian Dominican priest Gustavo Gutiérrez, Muslim romantic revolutionary Ali Shari'ati, and the prophetic activism of Noam Chomsky to theorize and/or practice a "liberation theology" as a form of revolt freed from religion. Now meet the three wise Magi: Henry David Thoreau, Mahatma Gandhi, and Martin Luther King, as through American transcendentalism they retrieve a collective memory from three Persian sages, Sa'di, Rumi, and Hafez. Yes, three wise Magi: Hemingway, Faulkner, and Steinbeck. You can take any of the myriads of prophets you like and give me the three wise Magi: Akira Kurosawa, John Ford, and David Lean—when they dreamed of empires they feared and fancied.

DOI: 10.1057/9781137301291

This is how we can—we must—re-world the world: through the wise magi we have had among us but were blinded to them—at one and the same time.

Being-in-the world with/out religion

First to quote and then to unquote religion as a fetishized commodity that had to compete for attention with other commodities of its own invention—secularism, modernity, the West—is to let it loose from its long incarceration in the hidden dungeons of dead and forgotten labor that is no longer glittering under the surface of the commodity and that has all but lost its organic link to the amorphous capital. We walk through Times Square and wonder, in a hall of mirrors where the society of spectacle has replaced the fetishized commodity, overcome it, a double negative, as a mere spectre of itself. We walk south from Times Square to the depleted site of the World Trade Center—a misnomer, for world trade no longer has, or did it ever have, a center—where the society of spectacle has had its historic rendezvous with religion as the metaphysics of violence. Those two tall totem poles and proud, phallic high-rises were so projected and powerful as they showed off their architectural embrace of engineering and industry, physics and poetry. And where they were cut down, by militant Muslims flying their manhood into an orgiastic spectacle so that the whole world could see their orgasmic gush, the location of castration was covered, curtained, and cordoned off. For no one should or could or would be allowed to see the location of the absence, where the manhood of "the West" was castrated from deep down in its groins. The excavated and covered site of the twin towers was no womb or vagina as some feminists suggest, unaware of an entirely homoerotic disposition to this masculinist warfare. On 9/11 the male Muslim militant was religion, and it slit the throat and cut the manhood of "the West," its own creator, its own father. September 11, 2001, was patricidal, the bastard son at once claiming and killing his father. This was no act of "deferred obedience," as Freud thought, but "deferred defiance," as we know it only too well on the colonial site of our emasculation. Religion, on the colonial site, is emasculation—as secularism is vicarious lovemaking—Mustafa Saeed of Tayeb Salih's *Season of Migration to the North* (1966) lobotomized like Stanley Kubrick's Alex DeLarge in *Clockwork Orange* (1971).

DOI: 10.1057/9781137301291

To quote and then to unquote religion is to retrieve the moment of its absence, when there was no name for it. In Islam, where I live, the bad Muslim that I am, and the belligerent Muslim that I have become since 9/11 in New York, *Din* for *faith* never meant much more than a state of being—impermanent, mimetically momentary (you go to sleep a mystic and wake up a philosopher, and you disregard the juridical nuisance of the clerics)—a pathway, a highway, or a byway that had Shari'ah, Tariqah, or Haghighah as its alternate routes, depending on how congested or hazardous the alternative roads were. This thing we call *din*, which I have a choice of not translating as "religion," was a map of multiple networks; no Muslim ever just took one road and went to the end. The polyfocality of the map made it possible to be-in-the-world without any declarations of fanatical fantasies or invincible principles. Our sort of mimetic mood, before what I now have the luxury of not calling "the West" turned us into "the Rest," was neither Aristotelian nor fixed. We were playful with our mimetic mannerism (code-named *Fiqh* one day, *Falsafeh* another, *Tasawwuf* the next)—doing one thing today and another tomorrow, or even on a given day philosophize as we breakfasted in the morning, pray and fish in the afternoon, read poetry and rear cattle in the evening, paint, do calligraphy and criticize after dinner, just as our distant German cousin had in mind, without ever becoming a philosopher, a hunter, a Sufi, a fisherman, a herdsman or a critic.

In what "Islam" and our cleric want all to themselves, we Muslims were not guided by our mimetic acts of affinity; they were mobilized by us, at our disposal. The nomocentricity of the Shari'ah Law that sought to legislate our bodies and behavior was modified by the logocentricity of the philosophical monkey wrench we threw at it, as our *Fiqh* and philosophy were both challenged, at times politically, by the homocentricity of our iconoclastic, defiant, bombastic Sufism, whose theoerotic disposition did not sit well with our doctors of law or masters of reason. On behalf of the West, a whole platoon of Orientalists invented Islamic, Chinese, or Indian civilization so that the West could believe in itself. Islam, before colonialism acted as a catalyst to turn it into militant Islamism, was more a systemic meandering in the cosmopolis of an emotive universe, when you could, as Marx fantasized, fish in the morning, rise up in a revolution in the afternoon, or, more likely, be a saintly Sufi and ask world conquerors on horseback for a favor, to step aside please and let the sunshine warm us up—in the timely scale of history.

DOI: 10.1057/9781137301291

Colonialism ended all that, placed a misplaced concreteness on an amorphous irreality and started name-calling Islam a religion. Colonialism angered Muslims into rebellion and turned them all to making a militant Islamism out of their scattered and misplaced pieties. By the same token (and in the same vein) that, in conversation with Greek philosophy Muslims had crafted their own philosophy; in conversation with Jewish theology, their own theology; and with Buddhism, their own mysticism, so, in combative conversation with European colonialism they turned their own ancestral faith into a colonized conception of their own faith, now code-named Islam, Islamism. Colonialism made an Islam out of people's varied pieties and then turned that Islam into a religion. When there was Islam there was no name for it; when Orientalism/colonialism made a name for it, there was Islamism—the nightmare of Islam of itself, under the gun barrel of (not Christianity), but colonialism. Israel is Judaism multiplied by colonialism equals Zionism. The Islamic Republic is Islam multiplied by the colonized mind of militant Muslims equals a theocracy. America is Christianity multiplied by imperialism equals Christian fundamentalism. Here are the three Abrahamic religions in their belligerent history, deprived of their worldliness and turned upside down into militant ideologies of war and conquest, war and domination, war and resistance. Commodities fetishized into an arsenal of ideological warfare.

In Iran, where I was born, Islam has always been integral to all phases of its unfolding cosmopolitan cultures, but never definitive of any one of them. Islamic civilization, which (along with Indian or Chinese civilizations) the European Orientalists invented in order to match and corroborate (though placed in the Hegelian infancy of world history) the equally vacuous coinage of the Western civilization, glossed over the fact and phenomenon of the polyfocality of that which was thus branded and named—or if we were to put it in Weberian terms rationalized, codified, and its chaotic confusions controlled. Islamic civilization coined and made current Islam and turned Islam into religion. Whereas religion is definitive and conclusive (demands and exacts finitude), the thing itself (which I have the choice of not calling din) is always already implicit, inconclusive, an *opera aperta* (as Umberto Eco would say), tangential, invisible and visible only through its varied forms of other-than-itself. The intentions of that which I have the choice of not naming Allah (author), the intentions of that which I have the choice of not calling the Qur'an (text), and the intentions of that which I have the choice of

DOI: 10.1057/9781137301291

calling Muslims—if Umberto Eco were to be borrowed and asked to lend a hermeneutic hand—would implicate an infinity of interpretive possibilities that all band together and run away from the rubric of Islam the instant we name it, and yet (how strange), it becomes palpable the instant we cease calling it names). The moment, the moment of an Islamic naming, an Islamic revolution, and Islamic republic, that it (*die dinge selbst*) was violently forced to become definitive, it stopped even being integral and people (Muslims—nominal, denominational, believing or otherwise) either openly revolted against their own faith, or else embraced it in ostentatious militancy, thus protesting too much. Militant Muslims protest too much because of their worldly whereabouts that they now dub religion and want to protect against the infidels and the apostates, or against what they have always already lost, or else against a phantom fear they keep calling "the West." And thus it was that the binary "Islam and the West" depleted the world of its worldliness (which included Islam, Christianity, and Judaism but not marked by any one of them) and replaced it with a malignant case of commodity fetishism that takes the fetish of the thing for the thing itself. When commodity fetishism becomes form, we are readied to move to the society of spectacle, where the form has become the image, the signifier sign, and violence iconic. September 11, 2001, was the spectacle of iconic violence, when violence ceased to be anywhere near its Weberian sociology of legitimacy or else part of a Fanonite politics of revolutionary decolonization—neither legitimate nor purposeful. For by now, Osama bin Laden was the sign of violence for spectacular and iconic reasons, violence as something to behold.

From muselmann to muslim, from umma to camp

Who inhabits the estranged and fetishized religion today, at its thither end? Muslims have become among the last denied, vestiges of the religious and the religion, and yet at the very same time Muslims have become (and thus revolt against) the historical updating of the German concentration camps figure of the *Muselmann*—the simulacrum of Man, the dead-man walking, the bare life, stripped of all worldly mannerism, civil liberties, and legal protections and taken for the naked violence the world suffers. The naked life, stripped of its civil liberties, that which Agamben trembled with philosophical fear when he made us see and recognize,

DOI: 10.1057/9781137301291

the concentration camp *Muselmann* walking into the streets and alleys of Western (as Agamben still calls it) law to occupy the state of exception in Guantanamo Bay, Bagram Airbase, and Abu Ghraib, quite ironically as a Muslim (a *Muselmanm*), as an enemy combatant, now beholden as both the epiphany of that iconic violence and as its primary target. The militant Muslim as enemy combatant (subject to the law but outside the law, at once lawless and illegal) is both the source and the immediate target of his own violence—suicidal violence. The body of the militant Muslim exploding itself in Iraq, Afghanistan, or Palestine is now the terra incognita of that violence, of a state shorn of or denied its territoriality (either occupied or stolen from under his and her feet) and reduced to the body of its first and final citizen, and of the body-politics that fails to inhabit or to govern it, and yet at the same time is at its mercy, and by way of denying the globalized and amorphous state the primary site of its violence it explodes itself.[6] The body of the self-exploded Muslim militant is now beyond the control of Weberian sultanism, beyond Harold Lasswell's garrison state, beyond Foucault's governmentality, beyond even Agamben's state of exception. For his state of exception has now become the rule, though not the law. Never the law.

As *bios* has become *zoë*, *Muselmann* Muslim, state sovereignty "the state of exception," nation-states camps, and violence iconic, religion, then, even as a trope, has devoured itself, become transparent for what it was (not). So the shredded body of the militant Muslim is the site of the last martyr, witness to its own absence, the vision of its own invisibility, the vista of its own disappearance, the first victim of his own last violence, the last simulacrum of humanity in a post-human body, only visible in the incandescent and immaterial visibility of an art and a poetry, a cinema and a photography that is all about him but never about him—the site and citation where we see religion bidding adieu to itself, as it is leaving the world in ruins, the final form of an immaterial, but palpable, gift of terrorizing grace.

As the world is distracted by the moral meltdown of religion, torn asunder by the warring factions of a Christian empire, a Jewish state, an Islamic republic, a Hindu fundamentalism, a Buddhist nationalism, all underlined by a militant secularism, our worldliness is held invisibly together by the anamorphic grace of an invisible and quiet certitude that has gotten lost, disguised in worldly matters, in visions of the invisible that we face and watch and allow to grace our lives without it ever announcing itself as religion. The world has overcome religion.

DOI: 10.1057/9781137301291

Wahdat al-Wujud

The paradox between the two moments when there was Sufism but there was no name for it and when there was a name for it but there was no Sufism dwells in the precise but lapsed instance of colonial naming when a happily free and floating sign is arrested, incarcerated, and told to sit down and behave, in one way or another. Just like a caught, pinned-down butterfly, and life and liberty (and what Hannah Arendt paraphrased as the pursuit of "public" happiness) is tortured out of its body and stolen from its soul, Sufism here stands for the thing that is always in a defiant mood, refusing naming, christening. Today religion stands between *die dinge selbst* (the thing itself) and the eye of the beholder. *To khodhejab-khodi*, says Hafez, *azmianbarkhiz* (you are the veil of yourself, Hafez/ remove yourself!)

Naming commences from a moment of fundamental distrust about being-in-the world, about the world, multiple worlds that we habitually inhabit—when and where the fear of chaos is infinitely more than the possibility of chaos, when and where the fear of flying makes you crawl. Un-naming the named restores that lost confidence in and about the world, embracing and even celebrating its fragile impermanence, very much the way Omar Khayyam enjoins that impermanence by at one and the same time noting and escaping it, celebrating and mourning the fragile grace of the world.

> For some we loved, the loveliest and best That from His rolling vintage Time has pressed, Have drunk their glass a round or two before, And one by one crept silently to rest.

Notes

1   Among his other works see Philip Rieff's *Fellow Teachers*(New York: Harper & Row, 1973). For an extension of Rieff's theory of culture to an Islamic/ Shi'i context see my *Shi'ism: A Religion of Protest* (Cambridge, MA: Harvard University Press, 2010).

2   See Gil Anidjar, "Secularism" (*Critical Inquiry*, 33: Autumn 2006)

3   See Talal Asad, *Genealogies of Religion: Discipline and Reasons of Power in Christianity and Islam* (Baltimore, MD: Johns Hopkins University Press, 1993).

DOI: 10.1057/9781137301291

4   In two successive moves—in *Theology of Discontent* (1993) and *Islamic Liberation Theology* (2009)—I have sought to document a history of this binary as two complementary bookend moments of colonial modernity.

5   Talal Asad, *Genealogies of Religion* op. cit.: 4.

6   For my reflections on suicidal violence see Hamid Dabashi, *Corpus Anarchicum: Political Protest, Suicidal Violence, and the Making of the Posthuman Body* (New York: Palgrave Macmillan, 2012).

DOI: 10.1057/9781137301291

Conclusion: Toward a Hermeneutics of Alterity

In this book I have tried to posit a hermeneutic of alterity as opposed to a metaphysics of identity as the manner of being a Muslim in the world. The absolutism of certainty within a metaphysical regime will have to be posited against the uncertainty of living it against the absolutist convictions of the other. Ultimately, the collapsing of the binary between "religion and secularity" and "Islam and the West" entails the necessity of thinking through a hermeneutics of alterity that will teach us how to live with uncertainties, in a world that only humanity can inhabit by virtue of the language that mediates that possibility. To rise to the post-Western world means to transcend the politics and ultimately the metaphysics of identity and reach for a hermeneutics of alterity.

To place the constitutional force of "Islam" in its cultural context and thus argue against the customary Islamicization of that cultural context, my principal argument has been that instead of an imaginary line called "Islam" encircling the multiple cultures it is supposed to embrace and define, it is those multiple cultures that have placed the Qur'anic and Muhammadan memories within themselves. My detecting a panorama of *worldly* sources of imagination in these cultures has been geared more towards a widening of our reading parameters of these cultures rather than positing a "secular" pole to the customary "sacred" basis of the Orientalist discourse on "Islamic societies."

By positing a hermeneutics of alterity, I have sought more to place "Islam" within a social and intellectual

DOI: 10.1057/9781137301291

history that embraces and animates it rather than questions the enduring significance that the Muhammadan revelation has had for that
history. My principal proposal has been that we will have a far sharper
view of the social and intellectual history of societies in which the
Muhammadan charismatic legacy has endured if we subject that endur-
ance to the multicultural parameters that have located and placed the
Qur'anic revelation in alternating contexts. These alternating contexts,
which I have designated via the articulation of a series of hermeneutic
moves, are *worldly* to the sacred centrality of the Qur'anic imagination.

Between faith and infidelity, or between the sacred certitude of its
metaphysics and the worldly sources of its creative imagination, a culture locates precisely that interpretative space where a hermeneutics of
alterity can detect and retrieve its unresolved problematic. Retrieving
the enduring problematic of a culture and engaging them in a way that
is true to historical exigencies is where a hermeneutics of alterity can
lead to an analytics of post-Orientalism. What is particularly evident
in the historical formation of the so-called Islamic culture, even if we
so identify it, is the creative tension that has always existed between its
theocentric and its anthropocentric forces, its centralizing proclivities
and its decentering energies. To be a Muslim in the world is to retrieve
that dialectic. To call that effervescent culture that is made by its active
hermeneutics of alterity "Islamic" (or "non-Islamic" for that matter)
is to deny that creative tension and thus to rob that culture of its most
vital energy. To put that creative tension back into the very fabric of the
varied cultures that produced and were in turn produced by it is what a
hermeneutic of alterity can begin to articulate and theorize.

In sum, the hermeneutics of alterity is a mode of interpretative apparatus that seeks a way out of the lapsed crisis of Orientalism—a mode of
knowledge that entrapped rather than emancipated. While Orientalism
wedded the colonial essentialism to the Enlightenment positivism to
generate consensus in matters of Oriental knowledge, the hermeneutics
of alterity I propose here opts for contestation as the principal mode of
operation in production of knowledge. "Contestation" is here operative
not only in the historical production of Muslim cultures in their plu-
ralities where opposing forces engage each other, but also in any hermeneutic access to the vital forces of those historical productions. Such sites
of opposition as *the sacred* and *the mundane* (the worldly), or the *juridical*
and the *mystical*, or the *rational* and the *inherited* are where cultures
expose their most vital energies. To understand a culture is to retrieve

DOI: 10.1057/9781137301291

those sites of opposition, to re-articulate its unresolved tensions. The crisis of Orientalism commenced from the fact that colonial knowledge was produced in order to control. The only way to resist post-colonial abuse of knowledge is, not to stop producing it, but to change the epistemic premise of knowledge production from consensus to conflict, from Orientalism to a hermeneutic of alterity that seeks, identifies, and retrieves the oppositional sites of cultural contestations. In between the opposing sites lies a vast and open-ended highway upon which Muslims see the expansive horizons of their being in the world.

DOI: 10.1057/9781137301291

Index

DOI: 10.1057/9781137301291

DOI: 10.1057/9781137301291

DOI: 10.1057/9781137301291

DOI: 10.1057/9781137301291

CPSIA information can be obtained at www.ICGtesting.com
Printed in the USA
LVOW08*1710170813

348395LV00005B/70/P